Great Adventures

HISTORY BITES

Solomon Schmidt

This book is dedicated to my parents for their unending love, support, and encouragement.

Also, to Paul, Saroj, Prem, and Avi for going above and beyond the call of duty to help me and my dad during our adventure in Nepal. And to Apa Sherpa, a legendary Everest climber, for his kindness and friendship to me and for his great efforts in promoting education among the Sherpa people.

Also, to the memory of mountaineering guide Rob Hall (1961-1996), who lost his life on Mt. Everest while trying to save one of his clients. And to his remarkable daughter, Sarah Arnold-Hall, who has encouraged and inspired me in my work.

And many thanks to Bill Potter and Cody Mitchell for their friendship, expertise, and insight.

Great Adventures History Bites includes thirty sections about some of the most fascinating and incredible adventures in world history. Many of the adventurers in this book are well-known historical figures, but others are not, even though they accomplished amazing things.

It is my hope that through reading this book, you will be inspired to learn more about all of these adventurers, the journeys and expeditions they took, and the places they explored.

Several facts in this book are not common knowledge and required citations. These can be found in the section "Works Cited" at the end of the book.

Also, special thanks to L.B. Dugan for the excellent maps she created for this book.

~Solomon

TABLE OF CONTENTS

☆☆☆☆☆☆☆☆☆☆☆☆☆☆☆☆

Viking ship off the coast of Greenland

The Vikings were a group of people from an area of land called Scandinavia, which includes the countries of Norway, Sweden, Denmark, Finland, and Iceland. Many people who lived near Scandinavia were afraid of the Vikings because they were fierce fighters who went on **raids** to other lands.

Erik the Red was a Viking from the island of Iceland, and he had a son named Leif, who was born sometime between **A.D. 960-980**. While growing up, Leif Erikson (Erikson means "Erik's son") learned how to read and write and also how to fight. Around A.D. 982, his father, Erik, got into an argument with another Viking and killed him. Because of this, Erik was **banished** from Iceland, and he sailed away with his family to find a new home. They eventually landed on the island of Greenland, where they built houses and planted crops.

Near the beginning of A.D. 1000, Leif Erikson sailed to Norway to visit Olaf Tryggvason, the king of Norway. King Olaf was a Christian, and he wanted Erikson to go back to Greenland to tell the Vikings about Christianity.

According to an **ancient** book called the *Saga of Erik the Red*, on his way back to Greenland, Erikson sailed into heavy winds on the Atlantic Ocean, and his ship was blown away from the direction of Greenland. He discovered a new land, which today is the continent of North America. Erikson landed in present-day Canada and named the new land "Vinland" because of the grapes that grew on vines there. He also discovered that Vinland had many trees, which the Vikings could use to build houses.

After spending time exploring this new land, Erikson and his **crew** sailed back to Greenland, and he told his family and the other Vikings about his discovery. Erikson stayed in Greenland for the rest of his life, and even though he did not return to Vinland, his sister, Freydis, led a group of Vikings to settle there. According to the *Saga of Erik the Red*, many of them were attacked and killed by Native Americans, and after this, no other Vikings settled in Vinland.

Leif Erikson was the first European to discover North America. His voyage to Vinland and exploration of that land was one of the greatest adventures in history.

Ruins of a Viking church in Greenland

Leif Erikson pointing to North America in the distance

Leif Erikson landing in North America

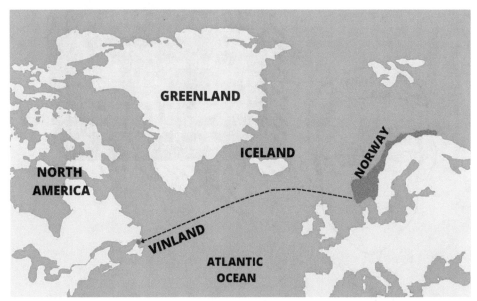

Map of Leif Erikson's voyage to North America by L.B. Dugan

REVIEW BITES

VOCABULARY

Raids – attacks in which people capture land and steal important items

A.D. – a term that stands for the Latin words *Anno Domini*, which mean "in the year of our Lord"; this term refers to all dates after the birth of Jesus Christ

Banished – forced to leave one's home or country as a punishment

Ancient – very old

Crew – a group of sailors who work together on a ship

FUN FACT

When he was young, Leif Erikson learned the stories and beliefs of the Vikings. One Viking belief was that the Earth was flat and that if you sailed too far, you would run into a huge sea monster named Jörmungandr, who surrounds the sides of the world.

REVIEW QUESTIONS

1. Who was Leif Erikson's father?

2. Why did King Olaf of Norway want Erikson to go back to Greenland?

3. What did Erikson name the land that he discovered in A.D. 1000?

1. Erik the Red 2. To tell the Vikings there about Christianity 3. Vinland

9

Journeys of Marco Polo
1271-1295

Marco Polo sailing back home to Europe

Marco Polo was born in the city of Venice, Italy, in 1254. His father, Niccolò, and his uncle, Maffeo, were **merchants**. When Marco was young, his father and uncle traveled to China and met Kublai Khan, who was the emperor of the Mongol Empire from 1260 to 1294.

The next time Niccolò and Maffeo went to China, they took Marco with them. At this time in history, people traveling from Europe to China had to go on foot, and this took a very long time. Marco, his father, and his uncle left Venice in 1271 when Marco was seventeen years old, and they journeyed over mountains and across deserts on a **route** called the Silk Road. This route was used by merchants to bring clothing, spices, and other supplies from Europe to Asia, or from Asia to Europe.

In 1275, after four years of traveling, the Polos finally made it to the city of Shangdu (or Xanadu), where Emperor Kublai Khan lived. Emperor Khan became friends with Marco and made him his official **representative**. Over the next sixteen years, Marco traveled throughout the Mongol Empire on royal business for Emperor Khan. He explored many lands, including present-day China, India, and Vietnam. During his travels, Marco saw millions of people and many different animals and also learned about the postal (mail) system of the Mongol Empire.

In 1291, Emperor Khan gave Marco, his father, and his uncle permission to return home to Italy. After saying goodbye to the emperor, they sailed from China to Persia (present-day country of Iran), and from there, they continued to Venice on foot. In 1295, they finally arrived back in Venice after being gone for twenty-four years.

Three years later, Marco was taken prisoner during a war between the Italian cities of Venice and Genoa, called the Second Venetian-Genoese War. Marco had been fighting for Venice, his home, and was captured by the Genoese (people from Genoa). During his time in prison, he wrote a book about his journeys in Asia, called *The Travels of Marco Polo*. This book helped many Europeans learn about the lands and peoples of Asia, and it also inspired other explorers like Christopher Columbus to go on their own travels.

Marco Polo's incredible journeys throughout Europe and Asia were some of the greatest adventures of all time. (You can learn more about Marco Polo in my book *In/Famous People History Bites Volume 1*.)

An area of land in present-day Pakistan that was once part of the Silk Road
© Shahid Mehmood (refer to page 205)

Marco Polo

Emperor Kublai Khan

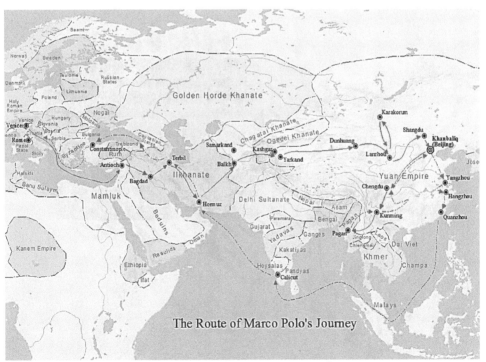

The Route of Marco Polo's Journey

Map of Marco Polo's journeys in Europe and Asia © SY (refer to page 205)

VOCABULARY

Merchants – people who buy and sell goods, such as clothing, jewelry, and food

Route – a road or path that people travel on

Representative – a person who speaks or does business for a leader/ruler

FUN FACT

One of the legends (fictional stories) about Marco Polo is that he brought back pasta from China to Italy and that is how it became a popular food there. That is actually false, but he did introduce the idea of using paper money in Europe after returning from his travels in Asia.

REVIEW QUESTIONS

1. How long did it take Marco Polo, his father, and his uncle to walk to China?

2. Whom did Marco work for during his journeys throughout the Mongol Empire?

3. What is the title of the book Marco wrote about his journeys in Asia?

1. Four years 2. Emperor Kublai Khan
3. The Travels of Marco Polo

Christopher Columbus landing in the present-day Bahamas

Christopher Columbus was born in 1451 in Genoa, Italy. As a young boy, he dreamed of exploring at sea, and so, he decided to work on a merchant ship to learn how to become a sailor. After reading *The Travels of Marco Polo*, Columbus wanted to journey to Asia himself. Instead of traveling by land like Marco Polo, he thought that he could reach Asia by sailing west on the Atlantic Ocean, which no one had ever done before.

During this time in history, people in Europe did not know that the **continents** of North and South America existed. Columbus believed that he would eventually land in Japan or China (referred to as the East Indies) if he sailed far enough west. However, he needed ships, food, and supplies to make this journey, and so, in 1484, he asked King John II of Portugal to **sponsor** his trip. Even though King John refused (said no), Columbus did not give up. After many years of asking King Ferdinand and Queen Isabella of Spain, they finally agreed to help Columbus and gave him three ships for his journey: the *Santa Maria*, *Niña*, and *Pinta*. They hoped that Columbus would find gold in Asia and that he would **convert** the Asian people to Christianity.

On August 3, 1492, Columbus and his crew set sail from Spain. They were not sure how far they had to sail, and they did not know what dangers they might face at sea. Columbus looked at the position of the sun, moon, and stars to **navigate**, and he kept a diary of what happened during each day of the voyage.

After two months of sailing, some of Columbus's crew were worried that they might not reach land and wanted to turn around and go home. Columbus told his crew that if they did not reach land in three days, they would return to Spain. Soon after that, on October 10, 1492, one of the sailors saw land in the distance, and on

October 12, Columbus and his crew landed on an island in the present-day Bahamas. At first, Columbus thought that he had reached the East Indies, and he named the native people on the island "Indians." Eventually, he realized that he had not sailed to the East Indies, but that he had actually discovered a new land, which is part of the present-day Caribbean Islands. This **region** became known as the New World.

Christopher Columbus became famous for his discovery of the New World, and King Ferdinand and Queen Isabella gave him the title "Admiral of the Ocean Sea." His first voyage to the New World was one of the greatest adventures of all time. (You can learn more about Columbus and his other voyages in my book *In/ Famous People History Bites Volume I*.)

Christopher Columbus's three ships sailing to the New World (from left to right: the Pinta, Niña, and Santa Maria)

Christopher Columbus talking with King Ferdinand and Queen Isabella

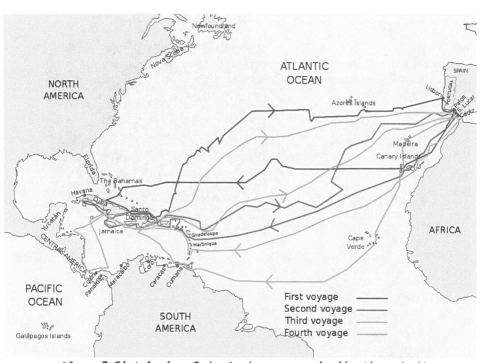

Map of Christopher Columbus's voyages to the New World
© Viajes_de_colon.svg: Phirosiberia (refer to page 206)

REVIEW BITES

VOCABULARY

Continents – very large areas of land; there are seven continents in the world: North America, South America, Europe, Africa, Asia, Australia, and Antarctica

Sponsor – pay for

Convert – cause someone to change their religious beliefs

Navigate – figure out the right way to go in order to reach a destination

Region – an area of land

FUN FACT

Christopher Columbus made three other voyages to the New World after his first one in 1492. He explored many lands in the present-day Caribbean Islands and Central America, including Cuba, the Dominican Republic, and Panama.

REVIEW QUESTIONS

1. Who gave Christopher Columbus three ships for his first voyage to the New World?

2. Where did Columbus and his crew land on October 12, 1492?

3. Where did Columbus think that he had landed?

2. On an island in the present-day Bahamas 3. East Indies
1. King Ferdinand and Queen Isabella of Spain

18

Vasco da Gama

One of Vasco da Gama's
ships sailing to India

Vasco da Gama was born sometime during the 1460s in the city of Sines, Portugal. Historians do not know much about his early life. His father, Estêvão da Gama, was the mayor (ruler) of Sines, and when he grew up, Vasco became a captain in the Portuguese navy and was well known for his leadership abilities.

At that time, merchants in Europe who wanted to journey to India had to do so by traveling over land. King Manuel I of Portugal wanted to find a way for Portuguese merchants to reach India by sea, and so, he put Vasco da Gama in charge of an expedition to sail to India.

On July 8, 1497, da Gama left Portugal and began his voyage to India with four ships and 170 sailors. He also brought along men who could speak the Arab language so that they could be **translators** on the expedition. It was a long and dangerous journey, and many of da Gama's men died along the way. By the end of July, da Gama and his crew reached the Cape Verde Islands, which are off the western coast of Africa. After this, they set out far into the South Atlantic Ocean. Da Gama wanted to stay away from an area in the ocean known as the Gulf of Guinea, where the **currents** could move his ships in the wrong direction.

On November 22, 1497, da Gama and his crew sailed around the Cape of Good Hope on the southern coast of Africa, which had been discovered in 1488. It was a very dangerous place because storms often formed there. Over the next few months, da Gama continued on his journey to India by sailing up the eastern coast of Africa. In April of 1498, he reached the city of Malindi in the present-day country of Kenya. While in Malindi, da Gama met a man who knew the way from Africa to India, and he joined the expedition.

After leaving Malindi, da Gama and his crew set sail across the Indian Ocean, and a few weeks later, they saw the Ghats Mountains of India in the distance. On May 20, they landed in the city of Calicut, India, and da Gama became the first explorer to sail from Europe to India. While in India, he met the ruler of Calicut, who was called the Zamorin, and he also found jewels and spices to take back to King Manuel of Portugal.

In August of 1498, da Gama left India and began the journey home. He sailed back around the Cape of Good Hope, and in September of 1499, he and his crew arrived in Portugal. Vasco da Gama became very famous because of his voyage to India, which was one of the greatest adventures in history. He eventually took two other voyages to India and died there in 1524.

Cape of Good Hope

Vasco da Gama landing in Calicut, India

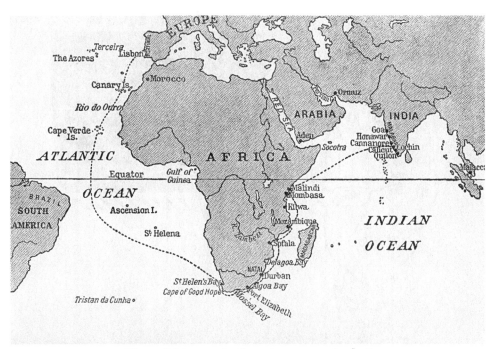
Map of Vasco da Gama's voyage to India

REVIEW BITES

VOCABULARY

Navy – a group of ships that is part of a country's military

Translators – people who explain the meaning of a language to someone who does not know how to speak it

Currents – water that moves in a specific direction

FUN FACT

A crater is a large hole created by a meteor (giant space rock) that crashes into the surface of a planet or moon. There is a crater on Earth's moon named after Vasco da Gama.

REVIEW QUESTIONS

1. What dangerous location on the southern coast of Africa did Vasco da Gama and his crew sail past?

2. Where did da Gama and his crew land on May 20, 1498?

3. Who was the first explorer to sail from Europe to India?

First Voyage Around the World
1519-1522

Ferdinand Magellan

Pacific Ocean

During the 1400s and 1500s, spices and jewels were worth a lot of money in Europe. One of the places people went to trade for these things was a group of islands called the Moluccas in present-day Indonesia, which are also known as the Spice Islands.

Ferdinand Magellan was born around 1480 in Portugal. He eventually became a sailor, and in 1505, he went on a voyage to the East Indies and spent many years in that region. After he returned to Europe, Magellan became excited about an idea he had for an expedition to the Spice Islands. Instead of sailing around Africa (like everyone else did at that time), he wanted to find a **passage** through South America and reach the Spice Islands by sailing west. King Charles I of Spain agreed to give Magellan five ships for his expedition.

On September 20, 1519, Magellan and his crew of 270 men set sail from Spain and began their voyage to the Spice Islands in five ships, which were named *Victoria, Trinidad, San Antonio, Conception,* and *Santiago.* After sailing for two months, they reached South America and traveled down the eastern coast of the continent. Magellan was trying to find the passage that he believed would lead them through to the other side of South America. After many months of searching, his sailors were nervous that they would never find this passage and that they would die at sea. Some of the crew took part in a **mutiny** against Magellan, but Magellan killed the leaders who started it and then continued on with his voyage.

At last, on October 21, 1520, Magellan and his crew entered a body of water that eventually became known as the Strait of Magellan. One month later, they reached the end of the strait and discovered a huge ocean in front of them. Magellan called it the *Mar Pacifico,* which means "peaceful sea" in the Portuguese language. Today it is known as the Pacific Ocean. At first, Magellan thought it would only take a short time for them to reach the Spice Islands. However, this new ocean was much larger than he had thought, and after weeks of sailing, their supplies were running out. His crew were eating rats to survive, and many were dying of disease and **starvation.**

After ninety-nine days of sailing across the Pacific Ocean, on March 6, 1521, Magellan and his crew discovered the island of Guam, where they loaded their ships with fresh food. About one month later, they landed on a group of islands called the Philippines. While there, Magellan and his crew got into a fight with some of the Philippine natives who refused to be ruled by the King of Spain. This fight is known as the Battle of Mactan. During the battle, on April 27, 1521, Ferdinand Magellan and many of his crew were killed by the Philippine natives. Some of Magellan's crew survived and escaped by boat. In November, they reached the Spice Islands and traded with the people there for spices and jewels.

By the time they left the Spice Islands, Magellan's crew only had one ship left (the *Victoria*). A man named Juan Sebastián del Cano had become the new leader of the expedition after Magellan was killed. Del Cano and his men began the long journey back to Spain, sailing across the Indian Ocean, around the Cape of Good Hope, and up the western coast of Africa.

On September 6, 1522, nearly three years after setting out, del Cano and his crew arrived back in Spain. Only eighteen of the 270 men who had begun the journey with Ferdinand

Magellan made it back alive. Their voyage around the world was one of the greatest adventures of all time, and it proved that planet Earth is round, not flat (which many people believed at that time in history).

Ferdinand Magellan landing in Porto Seguro, Brazil

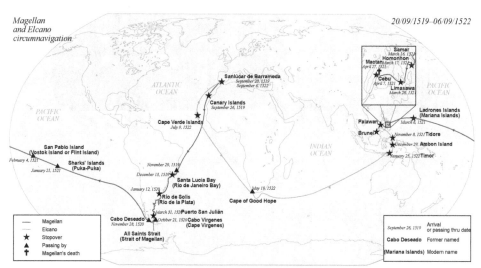

Map of the first voyage around the world
© Sémhur (refer to page 206)

REVIEW BITES

VOCABULARY

Passage – a waterway in the middle of an area of land that connects one body of water to another

Mutiny – a crew's rebellion against a sea captain

Starvation – when someone dies because they do not have enough food to eat

FUN FACT

During its voyage, the *Victoria* sailed a total of 42,000 miles, which is equal to traveling around planet Earth almost two times.

REVIEW QUESTIONS

1. Where did Ferdinand Magellan hope to sail to on his expedition?

2. What ocean did Magellan discover on his voyage?

3. How many of Magellan's crew made it back to Spain?

Journey of Álvar Núñez Cabeza de Vaca 1527–1536

Álvar Núñez Cabeza de Vaca with Native Americans

The southeastern region of the United States
was first discovered in 1513 by a Spanish explorer named
Juan Ponce de León. He named the place where he landed
Pascua Florida, which means "feast of flowers" in
Spanish. Today, it is known as Florida. In 1527, a Spanish
explorer named Pánfilo de Narváez began an expedition to
Florida to conquer it for Spain. A Spanish soldier named
Álvar Núñez Cabeza de Vaca worked as the **treasurer** for
the expedition.

On June 17, 1527, Narváez left Spain with five ships and around six hundred crew members and sailed to the island of Cuba in the Caribbean Sea. While in Cuba, they got caught in a **hurricane**. During the storm, two of the ships sunk, and hundreds of the crew members died.

In April of 1528, Narváez and his men set sail from Cuba and landed on the western coast of Florida. After weeks of exploring through swampy lands, they began running out of food and were also being attacked by Native Americans. Narváez decided to leave, but because he and his men had left their ships behind, they built five new ships and set sail from Florida. While traveling across the Gulf of Mexico, the men got caught in a huge storm, which separated the ships. During the storm, Pánfilo de Narváez's ship and two others disappeared. Narváez and the crew members on those ships were never seen again.

The other two ships were pushed by the storm toward present-day Galveston Island, Texas, where they landed on November 6, 1528. Only eighty members of the expedition had survived the storm, including the treasurer Álvar Núñez Cabeza de Vaca. They were now alone in a land that no one from Europe had ever explored and were very far away from where Spanish settlers lived in Mexico.

Over the next several years, de Vaca and the other members of the expedition lived with Native Americans on the coast of Texas. De Vaca worked as a doctor for the Native Americans and also traveled throughout Texas to trade for food with other Native American tribes. Eventually, though, de Vaca wanted to leave Texas and return home to Spain.

So, in 1534, he and three other members of the Narváez expedition **fled** Texas and journeyed for hundreds of miles through the deserts of present-day New Mexico and Arizona. They walked south along the western coast of Mexico, and after two years of traveling, on April 11, 1536, de Vaca and the three men finally met some Spanish settlers in Mexico. In July of that same year, they reached Mexico City, which today is the capital of Mexico.

Álvar Núñez Cabeza de Vaca became famous for his journey through the present-day United States and Mexico, which was one of the greatest adventures in history. In 1542, he published a book about his travels called *La Relación de Álvar Núñez Cabeza de Vaca*, which means "The Relation of Álvar Núñez Cabeza de Vaca" in Spanish.

Desert in present-day New Mexico,
where de Vaca and his companions traveled

Map of the Narváez expedition and de Vaca's journey

REVIEW BITES

VOCABULARY

Treasurer – a person who keeps track of the money for a group

Hurricane – a huge and violent storm that usually forms over the Caribbean Sea and the Gulf of Mexico

Fled – ran away or escaped from

FUN FACT

"Cabeza de Vaca" means "head of a cow" in Spanish. Some historians believe that one of de Vaca's ancestors, named Martín Alhaja, received this name after the Battle of Las Navas de Tolosa in 1212 between the Spanish and the Muslims. Supposedly, Martín placed the head of a cow on a secret road through the mountains so that the Spanish army would know which way to go in order to attack the Muslim army and take them by surprise.

REVIEW QUESTIONS

1. What job did Álvar Núñez Cabeza de Vaca have on the Narváez expedition?

2. Where did de Vaca live for many years with the Native Americans?

3. How many men journeyed with de Vaca through present-day New Mexico, Arizona, and Mexico?

Captain James Cook

HMS Resolution in front of
Table Mountain in South Africa

By the mid-1700s, every continent in the world, except
Antarctica, had been discovered by European explorers. At
that time in history, some people believed there was another
continent in the southern **hemisphere** that was bigger than
any other continent. They referred to it as *Terra Australis
Incognita*, which means "the unknown land of the south" in
Latin. This land does not actually exist, but in 1820, explorers
discovered Antarctica, which is located in the southern
hemisphere at the bottom of planet Earth.

James Cook was born in 1728 in England. He eventually
became a sailor in the British Royal Navy and fought in the

Seven Years' War (you can learn more about this war in my book *Major Wars History Bites*). Cook knew a lot about sailing, math, and science and was also a great leader. In 1768, the Royal Society, which is a group of **prestigious** scientists in England, made James Cook the commander of an expedition to the Pacific Ocean in order to do scientific research.

On August 25, 1768, Cook and his crew set sail from England on a ship called the HMS *Endeavour* ("HMS" stands for "His/Her Majesty's Ship"). They journeyed around the southern tip of South America and continued on to the island of Tahiti, where they **observed** the planet Venus in the sky. From there, they sailed to New Zealand, which had been discovered in 1642.

Over the next six months, Cook and his men explored the two main islands of New Zealand. In April of 1770, they sailed up the southeast coast of Australia and through the Great Barrier Reef, which is a large coral rock formation in the Pacific Ocean. In July of 1771, Cook and his crew arrived back in England and were celebrated as heroes throughout the country for their journey.

One year later, James Cook began a second voyage in hopes of discovering the land of *Terra Australis Incognita*. In July of 1772, he set sail from England with two ships: the HMS *Resolution* and the HMS *Adventure*. He sailed around the southern tip of Africa and then journeyed farther south into the Antarctic Ocean. After searching for many months, Cook concluded (decided) that *Terra Australis Incognita* did not exist and then sailed north to New Zealand. From there, he and his crew journeyed around the South Pacific Ocean and returned to England in July of 1775. Because of his accomplishments at sea, James Cook was promoted to the **rank** of captain and became a member of the Royal Society.

Captain Cook was only home for one year before he set off on his third (and final) voyage in 1776 with two ships: the HMS *Resolution* and the HMS *Discovery*. For many years, people had believed that a waterway existed in North America that connected the Pacific Ocean and the Atlantic Ocean. They called it the Northwest Passage, and Captain Cook hoped to find out if it really existed. In January of 1778, while on his way to the west coast of North America, he discovered present-day Hawaii, which he named the Sandwich Islands. From there, he and his crew journeyed to North America, and after sailing for months along the western coasts of present-day Canada and the United States, they were unable to find the Northwest Passage (which does not exist).

In early 1779, Captain Cook returned to the Sandwich Islands. On February 14, he got into a fight with the natives because they had stolen a boat from him, and during the fight, Captain Cook was killed. The rest of his crew sailed back to England, arriving there in October of 1780.

Captain James Cook's three voyages around the world were some of the greatest adventures of all time. (You can learn more about Captain Cook's life in my book *In/Famous People History Bites Volume I*.)

Captain Cook and his crew in Tahiti

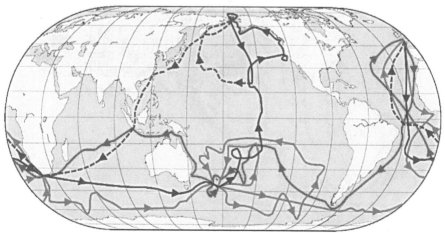

Map of Captain Cook's voyages (red line – first voyage, green line – second voyage, blue line – third voyage) © Jon Platek (refer to page 206)

REVIEW BITES

VOCABULARY

Hemisphere – one of the four main areas of planet Earth, which are: northern, southern, western, and eastern hemispheres

Prestigious – respected; important

Observed – watched from a distance

Rank – a position in the military

FUN FACT

The Maori are a group of people native to New Zealand whom Captain James Cook discovered when he explored there. The Maori had tattoos on their faces, and Captain Cook's sailors decided to get tattoos as well, but on their arms instead. This started a tradition that is still continued today by many sailors.

REVIEW QUESTIONS

1. Where did Captain James Cook and his crew observe the planet Venus on his first voyage?

2. What land did Captain Cook try to discover on his second voyage?

3. How did Captain Cook die in the Sandwich Islands?

1. Island of Tahiti 2. *Terra Australis Incognita*
3. He got into a fight with the natives there because they had stolen a boat from him, and during the fight, he was killed

Lewis and Clark Expedition
1804-1806

*Meriwether Lewis (left), William Clark,
and Sacagawea in present-day Montana*

Thomas Jefferson was the third president of the United
States, and when he became president in 1801, the thirteen
states in the United States only made up a small part of how
big the country is today. There was a large area of land to
the west of the United States called the Louisiana Territory,
which was owned by France. President Jefferson wanted to
make the United States a larger country, and so, in 1803, the
U.S. government bought the Louisiana Territory from French
Emperor Napoleon Bonaparte. (You can learn more about Napoleon
Bonaparte in my book *In/Famous People History Bites Volume I.*)

With this purchase of land, the United States became twice as big, and President Jefferson asked his **secretary** Meriwether Lewis to lead an expedition to explore the Louisiana Territory. With the help of an army officer named William Clark, Lewis organized a group of forty-eight men and three ships, and they became known as the **Corps** of Discovery.

The Lewis and Clark Expedition began on May 14, 1804, near St. Louis, Missouri, when the Corps of Discovery set sail on the Missouri River into the unexplored **wilderness** of western America. Over the next few months, they journeyed through present-day Missouri, Iowa, South Dakota, and North Dakota.

While in Iowa, on August 3, the expedition met two groups of Native Americans, named the Oto and Missouri **tribes**. They continued sailing up the Missouri River and eventually reached present-day Bismarck, North Dakota, where they met the Hidatsa tribe.

Because of the cold and stormy weather, Lewis and Clark could not continue their expedition during the winter months, and so, they built a fort and spent the months of November 1804 – April 1805 with the Hidatsa tribe. One of the Native Americans they met was a woman named Sacagawea, who knew the land out west very well, and she became a guide for the expedition.

By April of 1805, spring had arrived, and the expedition set out again on the Missouri River through North Dakota and into Montana. Lewis and Clark loaded one of their ships with plants and animals they had discovered and sent some men to take them back to President Thomas Jefferson in Washington, D.C. On May 26, 1805, Meriwether Lewis saw the Rocky Mountains in the far distance, and a few weeks later, the expedition came to the end of the Missouri River. In August, they crossed the Lemhi Pass in present-day Idaho and traded for horses with the Shoshone Native American tribe.

The expedition then journeyed over the Rocky Mountains and reached the Columbia River, which is on the border of Oregon and Washington and extends (continues) all the way to the west coast of the United States. The river was very fast-moving, and the expedition had to sail through stormy weather for several weeks.

At last, on November 15, 1805, the Lewis and Clark Expedition reached the Pacific Ocean and stood on top of the cliffs at a place called Cape Disappointment in Washington. They spent the winter of 1805–1806 at Fort Clatsop in Oregon, and in March of 1806, they set off to return home. On the way back, the expedition split up in order to explore more land: Meriwether Lewis journeyed on the Missouri River while William Clark sailed up the Yellowstone River through Wyoming and Montana.

After more than two years of exploring, on September 23, 1806, Lewis, Clark, and their men arrived back in St. Louis, Missouri, and they were celebrated as heroes throughout the United States. The Lewis and Clark Expedition was one of the greatest adventures in history, and it opened up many new areas of land for people in the United States to settle.

Lewis and Clark Expedition at the camp of the Shoshone tribe in Idaho

Map of the Lewis and Clark Expedition

REVIEW BITES

VOCABULARY

Secretary – a person who helps someone write letters and keep track of his/her schedule

Corps – a group of soldiers or explorers

Wilderness – a large area of land where very few people live (or none at all)

Tribes – groups of people who live together

FUN FACT

One of the animals that Lewis and Clark discovered on their expedition was the prairie dog, and they sent one back to President Thomas Jefferson as a present.

REVIEW QUESTIONS

1. What area of land did President Thomas Jefferson ask Meriwether Lewis to explore?

2. What mountain range did the Lewis and Clark Expedition travel over?

3. When did the Lewis and Clark Expedition reach the Pacific Ocean?

1. Louisiana Territory 2. Rocky Mountains 3. November 15, 1805

Sir Burton's Search for the Source of the Nile
1857-1859

Sir Richard Francis Burton

John Hanning Speke

The Nile River in Africa is the longest river in the world.
For many years, before Africa was made up of all the countries it
is today, people wanted to find out where the source (or, beginning)
of the Nile River was. One of these people was Richard Francis
Burton, who was born in 1821 in Great Britain. As a young man, he
became interested in other **cultures** and learned several languages,
including Latin, Greek, and French.

After studying at Oxford University from 1840-1842,
Burton joined the British Army and fought in India during a war
between Great Britain and a tribe called the Sindh. While in India,
Burton learned a lot about Asian and **Arabic** cultures, and he also

learned many new languages. He eventually returned to Great Britain and wrote several books about the peoples and lands he had seen during his time in India. Burton was tough and had a very adventurous spirit, and he wanted to explore the lands of Arabia and Africa. In the early 1850s, he took journeys to the Muslim city of Mecca in present-day Saudi Arabia and also to Somaliland in East Africa.

In 1856, with the help of the Royal Geographical Society in Great Britain, Burton began to organize an expedition to Africa to find the source of the Nile River. Together with a British explorer named John Hanning Speke, Burton traveled to the island of Zanzibar off the coast of East Africa. He hired over one hundred Africans and Arabs (people from Arabia) to help carry the food and supplies needed for the journey.

On June 5, 1857, Burton's expedition left Zanzibar and sailed to the coast of present-day Tanzania in Africa. From there, they began their journey through an area of the world that no other European had ever explored. The lands they traveled through were very hot, and Burton and Speke got sick with diseases that caused them to have fevers and go blind and even made them unable to walk at times. Along the way, they also **encountered** dangerous animals like hippopotamuses and poisonous snakes.

In November of 1857, Burton's expedition reached the city of Kazeh in Tanzania, which was ruled by Arabs. They were getting closer to a lake called Tanganyika, which Burton believed was the source of the Nile River. However, John Speke believed that another lake to the north (later named Lake Victoria) was where the Nile began. Because Burton was the leader of the expedition, they continued on to Lake Tanganyika instead of Lake Victoria.

On February 13, 1858, they reached Lake Tanganyika, which was very large, and Burton wanted to find out if the Nile River flowed out of it. However, he was very sick, and it was difficult for him to move. So, he sent Speke and several other members of the expedition in small boats to sail on the lake. During his time on Lake Tanganyika, Speke ran into many problems because he was not familiar with the lands around the lake, and he did not speak the languages of the native Africans who lived there. After exploring part of the lake, he eventually went back to Burton and told him that they had been unsuccessful in their search. Burton was very disappointed, and they had to turn around because they were running out of food and supplies.

During their journey back to the island of Zanzibar, Speke left the expedition for several weeks to find Lake Victoria, which he still believed was the source of the Nile River. He reached the lake on August 3, 1858, and then rejoined Burton's expedition in the city of Kazeh. From there, it took them another seven months to reach Zanzibar. In the spring of 1859, after almost two years of exploring in the wilderness of Africa, Burton and Speke sailed home to Great Britain.

John Hanning Speke eventually returned to Africa and proved that Lake Victoria was the main source of the Nile River by sailing from the lake into the river. Burton spent the rest of his life working for the British government and writing books about the people, lands, plants, and animals he had discovered on his journeys. In 1886, he was knighted by Queen Victoria for his many accomplishments (this means that he received the title "Sir" before his name). Sir Burton's search for the source of the Nile was one of the greatest adventures of all time.

Africans sailing on Lake Tanganyika

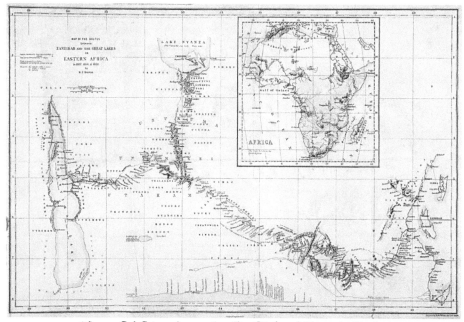

Map of Africa drawn by Sir Richard Francis Burton
Used by permission. © Special Collections, Princeton University Library

REVIEW BITES

VOCABULARY

Cultures – the customs and traditions of a people

Arabic – from the land of Arabia (present-day Middle East)

Encountered – came across

FUN FACT

Sir Richard Francis Burton could speak almost thirty languages, and by the end of his life, he had written over forty books and translated over thirty Asian and Arabic books into English, including *The Arabian Nights.*

REVIEW QUESTIONS

1. Why did Richard Francis Burton organize an expedition to Africa?

2. What British explorer traveled with Burton on his expedition?

3. Which African lake is the main source of the Nile River?

1. To find the source of the Nile River
2. John Hanning Speke 3. Lake Victoria

Burke and Wills Australian Expedition 1860-1861

Robert O'Hara Burke (pointing) and William Wills arriving at the Flinders River, near Australia's northern coast

After Captain James Cook sailed to the large island of Australia and said that it belonged to Great Britain (see Chapter 7: "Voyages of Captain Cook"), the British government began to use it as a place to send **criminals** because all of the prisons in Great Britain were full. Other people from Great Britain also journeyed to Australia to settle there and start new lives. By the mid-1800s, Australia was made up of several **provinces**, one of which was called Victoria. At that time, much of Australia had not been explored, and this unexplored land was known as the Outback.

In 1860, the leaders of the Victoria province hired a soldier named Robert O'Hara Burke to lead an expedition to explore the

Outback and reach the northern coast of Australia. They hired around twenty men to go with Burke and bought camels from India to help carry the water needed to cross the deserts in the Outback. A **surveyor** named William Wills was eventually made second-in-command of the expedition, which became known as the Burke and Wills Expedition.

On August 20, 1860, Burke and his men left Melbourne, the capital city of the Victoria province, and started on their journey to reach the Gulf of Carpentaria on the northern coast of Australia. It rained hard for many days, and the expedition moved slowly because the ground was very wet and muddy. Near the end of November, they arrived at a river called Cooper Creek, where they set up a camp near the present-day town of Nappa Merrie.

Burke was getting impatient with how slowly they were moving and wanted to reach the northern coast faster. So, while at their camp on Cooper Creek, he divided his expedition. He, William Wills, and two other men named John King and Charles Gray continued on. The rest of the men were told to wait at the camp for four months and then return to Victoria if Burke and his men did not return by then. On December 16, 1860, Burke, Wills, King, and Gray left the camp and began the last part of their journey to the northern coast. It was summertime in Australia, and the weather was hot. They crossed the Sturts Stony Desert and then reached the Selwyn Mountain Range. It was difficult for the camels they had brought to cross the mountains, but after several hard days, on January 21, 1861, Burke and his men made it through the mountains.

As they got closer to the northern coast, the weather became rainy, and there were many days in which they moved slowly through deep mud. On February 9, Burke and his men were very close to the northern coast, however, they could not pass through the thick forests and swamps that surrounded the beaches on the Gulf of Carpentaria. Because of this, they never got an open view of the ocean, and they turned around to return to the camp by Cooper Creek.

By this time, Burke and his men were starting to run out of food and eventually had to eat their camels and plants from the wild in order to stay alive. On April 16, Charles Gray died of starvation. Five days later, Burke, Wills, and King finally arrived back at their camp by Cooper Creek, hoping to find the men they had left there four months earlier. However, after waiting as long as they could, the men had left the camp just hours earlier that same day to return to Victoria. Burke, Wills, and King were now stuck alone in the Outback and were getting weaker each day from not having enough food to eat. Sadly, near the end of June, Burke and Wills both died of starvation, and in order to survive, King went to live with the native people of Australia, called the Aborigines.

Meanwhile, after not hearing any word from Burke and Wills for a long time, the leaders of Victoria had sent men to try to find them. In September of 1861, these men discovered John King living with the Aborigines and found Burke's and Wills's bodies, which were eventually brought back to Melbourne and buried. They also explored much of Australia and discovered important information about areas of land where people could settle and live in the Outback.

Robert O'Hara Burke and William Wills were the first people to journey across Australia from the southern coast to the northern coast. Even though it ended tragically, their Australian expedition was one of the greatest adventures in history.

Burke and Wills Expedition starving at their camp by Cooper Creek

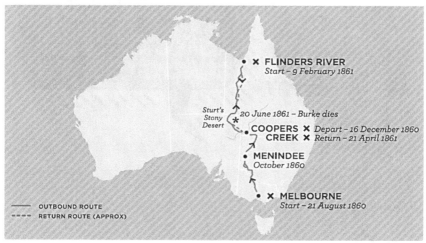

Map of the Burke and Wills Expedition
Used by permission. © Australian Museum

REVIEW BITES

VOCABULARY

Criminals – people who break the law and have to go to prison

Provinces – areas of land that are parts of a country (similar to states)

Surveyor – someone who explores areas of land and makes maps of those areas

FUN FACT

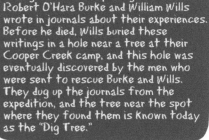

During their time exploring Australia, Robert O'Hara Burke and William Wills wrote in journals about their experiences. Before he died, Wills buried these writings in a hole near a tree at their Cooper Creek camp, and this hole was eventually discovered by the men who were sent to rescue Burke and Wills. They dug up the journals from the expedition, and the tree near the spot where they found them is known today as the "Dig Tree."

REVIEW QUESTIONS

1. What was the name of the large, unexplored area of land in Australia that the Burke and Wills Expedition was sent to explore?

2. Why did Robert O'Hara Burke divide his expedition?

3. How did Burke and Wills die?

1. The Outback 2. Because he got impatient and wanted to reach the northern coast of Australia faster 3. Starvation

John Wesley Powell

Disaster Rapids in Colorado

At the time of the American Civil War (1861-1865), the United States was around half the size it is today, and many people were leaving the eastern United States to settle in the west. As people continued to move west, more land was organized into states and added to the United States. By 1869, there was still one large area of land in the west that had not been explored: the Grand **Canyon**, which is located in the state of Arizona. This canyon is 277 miles long and over 6,000 feet deep at its deepest point. The Colorado River runs through the canyon, and the canyon is surrounded by desert lands.

John Wesley Powell was a **geologist** from New York, and during the 1850s, he went on scientific expeditions on the Mississippi and Ohio Rivers. He fought for the Union during the American Civil War and lost his right arm while fighting in the Battle of Shiloh. (You can learn more about the Civil War in my books *U.S. History Bites* and *Major Wars History Bites*.) After the war, Powell began teaching science at Illinois Wesleyan University, and in 1867, he took a trip to Colorado, where he climbed a famous mountain called Pikes Peak.

In 1869, Powell and nine men set out on an expedition to explore the Grand Canyon. On May 24 of that year, Powell's expedition left the town of Green River, Wyoming, and began rowing in four boats down the Green River. They packed food and supplies to last for one year and hoped to travel all the way to the Gulf of California in Mexico.

While on their expedition, Powell and his men had to sail through hundreds of **rapids**, and they were far from any city or town that they could get to if things went wrong. On June 9, something did go very wrong. While Powell's expedition was trying to sail through Disaster Rapids in Colorado, one of the boats smashed into a rock and broke apart. The men onboard survived, but many of the food and supplies for the expedition were lost.

Over the next six weeks, Powell's expedition continued down the Green River, passing through Desolation Canyon. In mid-July, they reached the point in Utah where the Green River flows into the Colorado River, and on August 5, they arrived at the beginning of the Grand Canyon. Powell kept a journal throughout the expedition and wrote about how amazed he was at the size and beauty of the canyon. He wanted to complete their journey and sail through the rest of the canyon, however, they were running out of food and supplies. Near the end of August, they reached a place that was later named Separation Rapids, and while there, three of the men on the expedition refused to go any farther. They climbed up the cliff wall of the Grand Canyon and out into the deserts that surround the canyon, hoping to reach a town that was seventy-five miles away. They were never seen again.

Meanwhile, Powell and the rest of his men continued rowing down through the canyon, and on August 30, they arrived at the place where the Colorado River and the Virgin River meet. Here they encountered **Mormons** from a nearby town who had heard about Powell's expedition. They thought that Powell and his men had died while journeying through the Grand Canyon. The Mormons gave Powell and his men food and shelter. Powell then traveled on horseback to Salt Lake City, Utah, and from there, he returned to the eastern United States. The men on his expedition, however, decided to stay out west and start new lives there.

John Wesley Powell's Grand Canyon expedition was one of the greatest adventures in history. Powell became known as a hero throughout the United States and was very influential in helping the U.S. government learn more about the lands out west. He died in 1902 in the state of Maine.

The Colorado River flowing through the Grand Canyon

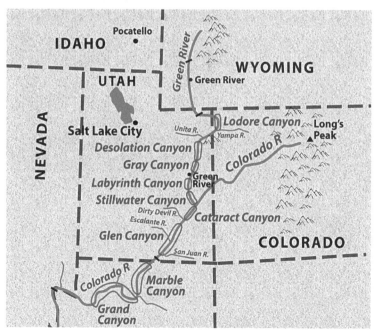

Map of Powell's 1869 Grand Canyon Expedition
Used by permission. © Ron Watters

REVIEW BITES

VOCABULARY

Canyon – a deep, long valley between mountains or hills

Geologist – someone who studies water, land, and rocks

Rapids – fast-moving parts of a river

Mormons – followers of Mormonism, which is a religion started by Joseph Smith (you can learn about Joseph Smith in my book *In/Famous People History Bites Volume I*)

FUN FACT

There are several places in the United States named after John Wesley Powell, including Mount Powell in California, the city of Powell, Wyoming, and Lake Powell on the border of Utah and Arizona.

REVIEW QUESTIONS

1. What state is the Grand Canyon located in?

2. What was the name of the place where John Wesley Powell's expedition lost one of their four boats?

3. How many men refused to go any farther once Powell's expedition reached Separation Rapids?

1. Arizona 2. Disaster Rapids in Colorado 3. Three

Stanley's Search for Dr. Livingstone
1871

Henry Morton Stanley meeting Dr. David Livingstone (in black clothes)

Dr. David Livingstone was an explorer and **missionary** from Great Britain, and during the mid-1800s, he went on several expeditions to Africa. He wanted to tell the native African tribes about Christianity and also wanted to help bring an end to the **slave trade** in Africa. Dr. Livingstone explored areas of land where no European had ever been, and he discovered Victoria Falls in the present-day country of Zambia. On one of his expeditions in 1844, he was attacked by a lion, which bit and seriously injured his left arm.

In 1866, Dr. Livingstone began an expedition to find the source of the Nile River. (Even though John Hanning Speke had discovered that Lake Victoria was the main source of the Nile, some people believed he was mistaken and that the true source had still not been found.) Dr. Livingstone's expedition encountered many problems, and his men eventually **deserted** him. By 1869, no one had heard anything from him for a very long time, and people around the world wanted to know what had happened to him. That same year, James Bennett, who was the owner of the *New York Herald* newspaper, decided to send a **journalist** named Henry Morton Stanley to find Dr. Livingstone. Stanley was from Great Britain but had moved to the United States in 1859 and fought in the American Civil War.

On January 6, 1871, Stanley arrived on the island of Zanzibar off the coast of East Africa. There, he bought the supplies he needed for the expedition. No one was exactly sure where Dr. Livingstone was (or if he was still alive), but Stanley's plan was to journey west into Central Africa to the town of Ujiji, where Dr. Livingstone had spent time on his expeditions. In February, Stanley sailed to the city of Bagamoyo on the coast of present-day Tanzania. While there, he organized a group of Africans and Arabs, along with donkeys and horses, to join him on the expedition. On March 21, Stanley's expedition set off into the wilderness of Tanzania, and throughout April, they faced rainy weather and had to travel over wet, muddy ground in the Makata Swamp.

After making it through the swamp, Stanley's expedition journeyed towards an area of land called the Ugogo Region. The weather changed and became very hot, with the temperature rising to 128 degrees Fahrenheit. Some of Stanley's men did not want to continue on and deserted the expedition. Near the end of June, Stanley and the men who stayed with him arrived at the city of Tabora, and they stayed there for three months. While in Tabora, Stanley got sick with cerebral malaria, which made him unable to think clearly. He also got smallpox, which is similar to (but worse than) the flu. By the end of September of 1871, Stanley was well enough to continue the search for Dr. Livingstone. He and his men left Tabora and traveled south in order to stay away from an area where a war was being fought between African tribes. The lands they traveled through were filled with many scary animals, and lions sometimes came near their camp at night.

Eventually, Stanley's expedition reached the Malagarasi River near Ujiji, which was full of crocodiles. They sailed across the dangerous river, and once they reached the other side, they met a man who told them that there was a white-skinned person in Ujiji. Stanley was very excited because he believed that this person was Dr. Livingstone. He led his men as fast as he could towards Ujiji, which is on the shores of Lake Tanganyika.

Around October 27, 1871 (historians are not sure of the exact date), Stanley's expedition arrived in Ujiji, and they were met by a white man with a thick beard. Stanley shook the man's hand and said, "Dr. Livingstone, I **presume**?" They had finally found Dr. Livingstone, who had spent the last few years living with Africans and Arabs and begging for food.

The news that Stanley's expedition had found Dr. Livingstone spread around the world. Dr. Livingstone still hoped to find what he thought was the true source of the Nile River and stayed in Africa until his death in 1873. Henry Morton Stanley returned to Great Britain and eventually led several more expeditions in Africa before he died in 1904. His search for Dr. Livingstone was one of the greatest adventures of all time, and the phrase "Dr. Livingstone, I presume?" became very famous.

Wilderness of Tanzania

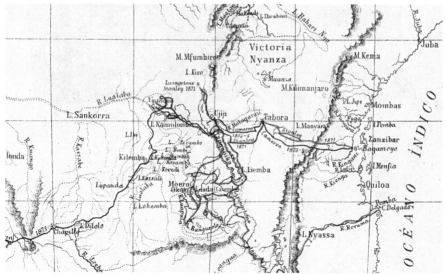

Map of Stanley's journey to find Dr. Livingstone

REVIEW BITES

VOCABULARY

Missionary – someone who goes to other countries to tell people about their religion

Slave trade – the practice of buying and selling people to work as slaves

Deserted – left alone

Journalist – someone who writes articles for a newspaper

Presume – when a person believes that something is true, but does not know for sure

FUN FACT

Henry Morton Stanley's favorite donkey on his expedition was named Simba, which means "lion" in the African language Swahili. This is also the name of the main character in the Disney movie *The Lion King*.

REVIEW QUESTIONS

1. Why did Henry Morton Stanley lead an expedition into Africa in 1871?

2. How long did Stanley's expedition stay in Tabora, where Stanley was very sick?

3. What famous words did Stanley say to Dr. David Livingstone when they met in Ujiji?

1. To find Dr. David Livingstone, who had been missing for years 2. Three months 3. "Dr. Livingstone, I presume?"

Captain Webb's Swim Across the English Channel
1875

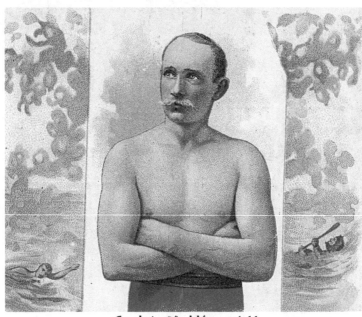

Captain Matthew Webb

The English Channel is a body of water between England and France, and it is about 150 miles long at its widest section and 565 feet deep at its deepest point. During England's summer season from June to August, the temperature of the water is usually around sixty degrees Fahrenheit. **Tides** and currents change the way the water moves through the channel each day. By the mid-1800s, many boats had crossed the English Channel, but no person had ever swum across it.

Matthew Webb was born in 1848 in Dawley, England, and as a boy, he learned to swim in the Severn River. He became a strong swimmer and even saved his brother Henry from drowning when they were young. In April of 1873, he was working on a steamship called the *Russia* which sailed from New York City to Liverpool, England. During the voyage, he jumped overboard into the ocean to try to save a drowning man, who disappeared into the water before Webb could save him. Even still, Webb became famous in England for his bravery, and around two years later, he began working as the captain of a steamship called the *Emerald*. Around this time, Captain Webb heard about a man named J.B. Johnson who had tried to swim across the English Channel in 1872, but had given up shortly after starting. Captain Webb decided that he was going to try to swim across the channel. In June of 1875, he quit his job on the *Emerald* and began to train in the Thames River in England.

People all over England heard that Captain Webb was going to try to swim across the English Channel. On August 12, 1875, he started his swim, but had to stop because of bad weather. Then, at 12:56 p.m. on August 24, Captain Webb jumped off Admiralty Pier in Dover, England, and began his long swim to France on the other side of the channel. He was wearing a pair of red shorts and had covered himself in porpoise oil, which would help him move smoothly through the water. Men in three small boats stayed near him to give him food and coffee during his swim.

Captain Webb was making good **progress**, and then, a jellyfish stung him in the shoulder. The men on the boats gave him a liquid called brandy to put on his shoulder so that he would not feel the pain from the sting as much. Captain Webb continued swimming towards France, but more slowly than before.

The water was calm that night, and the moon came out and shined over the English Channel. Every so often, boats carrying people between England and France would pass by Captain Webb, and the passengers on board would cheer for him to keep going. In the early hours on the morning of August 25, the wind picked up, and the water became rough as he got closer to Cape Gris-Nez on the coast of France. Captain Webb was very tired from swimming against the waves, which crashed into him and made him lose part of his sight in one eye. Even though he was weak, he kept going, and when the sun rose, he and his men saw France in the distance.

After swimming almost forty miles, at 10:41 a.m. on August 25, Captain Webb reached the shore at Calais, France, and became the first person to swim across the English Channel. Over the next several years, he took part in swimming competitions in England and the United States. In July of 1883, Captain Webb tried to swim through the rapids and **whirlpool** at Niagara Falls in the United States. However, the water was very powerful and fast moving, and sadly, he disappeared under the waves and died.

Captain Matthew Webb's swim across the English Channel was one of the greatest adventures in history, and it was not until 1911 that another person was able to swim across the channel.

Captain Webb pausing for a drink of coffee during his swim across the English Channel

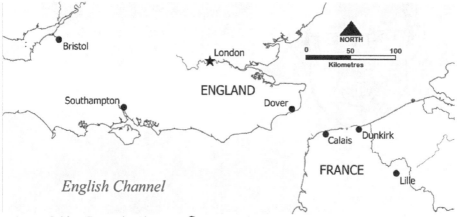

Map of the English Channel © Serial Number 54129 (refer to page 206)

REVIEW BITES

VOCABULARY

Tides – changes in the height of the oceans; high tide is when water levels are higher and cover more of a beach, and low tide is when water levels are lower and more of a beach can be seen

Pier – a platform that starts on land and goes out into the water

Progress – movement toward finishing a project or accomplishing something

Whirlpool – an area in a river or ocean where water swirls around and pulls things into it

FUN FACT

After Captain Matthew Webb became the first person to swim across the English Channel, people all over the world heard about his accomplishment. A drawing of him began to appear on items like dinner plates and match boxes.

REVIEW QUESTIONS

1. Which two countries is the English Channel located between?

2. What stung Captain Matthew Webb during his swim across the English Channel?

3. How many miles did Captain Webb swim to cross the channel?

1. England and France 2. A jellyfish 3. Almost forty

Thomas Stevens

Thomas Stevens in Japan

The bicycle was invented in 1817 by a German man named Karl Drais, and by the late 1800s, bicycles had become popular in the United States. There were different kinds of bicycles, including one known as the penny-farthing, which had a large wheel in front and a tiny wheel in back. Even though it was difficult to ride, it was the main bicycle that people used until the 1880s when another kind of bicycle was invented called the safety, which had two wheels that were the same size and was similar to the bicycles people ride today.

Thomas Stevens was born in 1854 in Great Britain, and he eventually moved to the United States, where he worked at different jobs in California, Wyoming, and Colorado. He learned how to ride a bicycle in San Francisco, California, and while working in a mine in Denver, Colorado, he had an idea to ride a bicycle across the United States. In 1884, he bought a penny-farthing bicycle, and on April 22 of that year, he left San Francisco on his bicycle and set off on his journey with a gun, a few clothes, and a raincoat that he used as a tent and a blanket. In May, he crossed the Sierra Nevada Mountains and biked through Nevada, Utah, and Wyoming. Along the way, Stevens stopped to meet with people from different bicycle clubs, and in June, he traveled through the Great Plains area of the United States, including Nebraska and Iowa. There were times when the weather was bad, and he had to stop and wait for it to turn nice.

In July of 1884, Stevens rode through the states of Illinois, Indiana, Pennsylvania, and New York. On August 4, he arrived in Boston, Massachusetts, and completed his ride across the United States. While he was there, Colonel Albert Pope, who owned a bicycle company, told Stevens that he would sponsor (pay for) Stevens to ride a bicycle around the world. Stevens agreed to do it, and in April of 1885, he sailed to England and planned his long journey. On May 2, he rode out of Liverpool, England, and bicycled to Croydon, England, where he sailed on a boat across the English Channel to France.

Over the next two months, Stevens took an exciting ride across Europe, traveling through the countries of France, Germany, Austria, Hungary, Serbia, and Bulgaria. In early July, he reached Constantinople (present-day Istanbul), which is the capital city of Turkey. After spending one month there, Stevens left Constantinople and rode through Turkey, Armenia, and Iraq. On September 30, he arrived in the city of Tehran, Iran. The Shah (or ruler) of Iran heard about Stevens's journey and invited him to spend the winter of 1885-1886 in Tehran as his special guest.

On March 10, 1886, Stevens set off on the most dangerous part of his journey. After bicycling through Iran, he tried to pass through the country of Afghanistan, but soldiers there **arrested** him and forced him to turn around. He then went back to Constantinople and sailed to the city of Lahore on the western coast of India, where he landed on August 1. Stevens enjoyed his ride through India, and he visited a famous **tomb** called the Taj Mahal in the city of Agra. On September 17, he left India on a boat that was sailing to southern China.

At that time in history, China and France were enemies, and during Stevens's bicycle ride through China, a group of Chinese people mistakenly (wrongly) thought that he was French. They tried to attack him, and Stevens had to ride for his life and hide in a field of bamboo plants. After riding for one month through China, Stevens reached the city of Shanghai on the eastern coast of China. From there, he sailed across the East China Sea to Nagasaki, Japan, for the last part of his journey.

His ride through Japan was very peaceful, and on December 17, 1886, he reached the city of Yokohama on the eastern coast of Japan. At last, he had finished his incredible journey and became the first person to ride a bicycle around the world. In all, he had ridden 13,500 miles.

Thomas Stevens lived many more years and traveled to Africa, Russia, and India and met famous people like Russian author Leo Tolstoy and Henry Morton Stanley (see Chapter 12: "Stanley's Search for Dr. Livingstone"). He died in 1935 in London, England, and his bicycle trip around the world was one of the greatest adventures of all time.

Thomas Stevens bicycling toward the Taj Mahal in India

Map of Stevens's bicycle journey © Benutzer: Dravot (refer to page 207)

REVIEW BITES

VOCABULARY

Mine – a place where things like gold, coal, and salt are dug out of the ground

Clubs – groups of people who get together to do activities

Arrested – when a person is taken by the police or military and is not allowed to go free for a certain amount of time

Tomb – a place where a dead person is buried

FUN FACT

While he was bicycling through the state of Nevada, Thomas Stevens encountered a mountain lion that was getting ready to attack him. Stevens shot a bullet at the lion, and even though he missed, the lion ran back into the woods. Thomas Stevens wrote about this and other adventures he had in a book called *Around the World on a Bicycle*, which was published in two parts in 1887 and 1888.

REVIEW QUESTIONS

1. Where was Thomas Stevens working when he had an idea to ride a bicycle across the United States?

2. What country did Stevens get arrested in?

3. Why did a group of Chinese people try to attack Thomas Stevens?

1. A mine in Denver, Colorado 2. Afghanistan
3. At that time in history, China and France were enemies, and the
Chinese people mistakenly thought that Stevens was French

Robert Peary with sled dogs
on board the Roosevelt ship

Peary's expedition at the North Pole

By the beginning of the 1900s, the only areas of the world that had not been explored were the Arctic and Antarctica. The Arctic is the area of land on the top of the world and includes parts of Canada and Greenland. The North Pole is the point in the exact center of the Arctic and is located at the very top of planet Earth. Most of the Arctic is made up of ice that covers the Arctic Ocean, and the weather there is usually very cold. No one lives in the areas right around the North Pole, but the Inuit (also known as Eskimos) are a group of people who have lived for hundreds of years in Canada and Greenland.

Robert Peary was born in 1856 in Cresson, Pennsylvania. When he grew up, he became a **civil engineer** in the United States Navy, and during the 1880s, he became very interested in the Arctic region. In 1886, Peary visited Greenland and got excited about the idea of exploring the Arctic. Over the next twenty years, he made several trips to Greenland and Canada, and during these trips, he started to make plans for a journey to the North Pole, which no one had reached. In 1905, Peary began an expedition to the North Pole, but the weather in the Arctic was so bad that he had to turn around soon after he began.

Then, on July 6, 1908, Peary and his crew left New York City on a ship called the *Roosevelt*, which had been built strong enough to break through ice in the North Atlantic Ocean. Peary and his men sailed to Cape York, Greenland, where several Eskimos joined the expedition. From there, they sailed to Ellesmere Island in Canada and set up a camp near Cape Columbia on the northern coast of the island. They spent the winter months of 1908-1909 there and gathered food, supplies, and animals that they would need for the expedition. Peary's plan was to divide his men into five groups, with each group going part of the way to the North Pole and setting up camps along the way. Once a group had finished setting up a camp, they would return to Cape Columbia, and the next group would pick up where the previous group had left off.

On February 15, 1909, the first group of Peary's expedition left Cape Columbia and began the journey over the frozen Arctic Ocean toward the North Pole. The men in each group wore thick fur coats and rode on sleds that were pulled by husky dogs. The temperature was very cold, sometimes dropping to more than sixty degrees below zero, and the winds blew hard. Every now and then, the temperature would get a little warmer, and because of this, parts of the ice would start to melt and break apart.

One day, Peary was sleeping in his **igloo** near one of the five groups of his expedition, and he heard shouting outside. When he came out, he saw that the chunk of ice his men had built their igloos on had broken off from the main section of ice that Peary's igloo was on. They started to float away, but thankfully, the water pushed them just close enough to the main section of ice that they were able to get back to safety.

During March of 1909, Peary's expedition continued to get closer to the North Pole, and one by one, the first four groups returned to Cape Columbia. Eventually, only Peary's group was left, and it included Peary, his friend Matthew Henson, and four Eskimos. On April 6, 1909, they arrived at the point on the very top of planet Earth, and Peary became the first person to reach the North Pole. His years of exploring and planning had finally paid off. Peary placed an American flag on the North Pole, and then he and his group journeyed back to Cape Columbia.

Robert Peary became known around the world for his expedition to the North Pole, which was one of the greatest adventures in history. The U.S. Navy gave him the important title of Admiral to honor him for his courage and perseverance on the expedition. He died in 1920 at the age of sixty-three in Washington, D.C.

Ice covering the Arctic Ocean

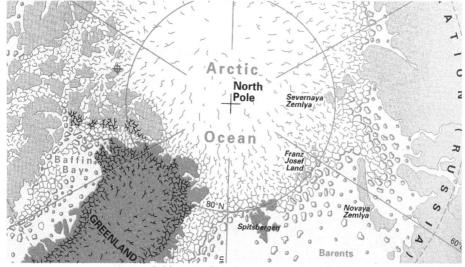

Map of the Arctic Ocean and North Pole

REVIEW BITES

VOCABULARY

Civil engineer – a person who designs plans for bridges, roads, and buildings

Igloo – a small, dome-shaped house made out of hard snow and ice

FUN FACT

Robert Peary was good friends with U.S. President Theodore Roosevelt. In 1908, before he sailed to the Arctic for his North Pole expedition, Peary visited President Roosevelt at his home on Long Island, New York. President Roosevelt gave Peary his best wishes for the expedition.

REVIEW QUESTIONS

1. What is the North Pole?

2. What group of people have lived for hundreds of years in Canada and Greenland?

3. What did Robert Peary place on the North Pole?

1. The point in the exact center of the Arctic located at the very top of planet Earth 2. The Inuit (also known as Eskimos) 3. An American flag

Captain Robert Falcon Scott

Roald Amundsen

Antarctica is one of the seven continents and is located on the bottom of the world. It is made completely of ice and is the coldest place on Earth, and because of this, no people group has ever made it their home. The South Pole is the point in the center of Antarctica, and it is located at the very bottom of planet Earth. Antarctica was discovered in 1820, but it was not until the early 1900s that people began to explore farther into the continent.

Robert Falcon Scott was a captain in the British Royal Navy, and he first traveled to Antarctica in 1902. He wanted to become the first person to reach the South Pole. In 1910, he sailed to Antarctica on a ship called the *Terra Nova* with around sixty men and many ponies, dogs, and sleds that were going to be used to move supplies. Captain Scott's expedition eventually reached the Ross Sea in Antarctica and set up a camp at Cape Evans.

At the same time, a man named Roald Amundsen was also trying to become the first person to reach the South Pole. He was an explorer from Norway and had spent many years sailing in Antarctica and the Arctic. In 1910, he left Norway on a ship called the *Fram* with around twenty men and sled dogs and sailed to the Bay of Whales in Antarctica. Along the way, Amundsen sent a **telegram** to Captain Scott to let him know that he and his men were also sailing to Antarctica to try to reach the South Pole. The race was on! Amundsen's expedition set up a camp on the Bay of Whales and began to pack the food, clothes, and supplies they would need for the journey.

One of the **advantages** that Amundsen's expedition had over Captain Scott was that Amundsen had made sure all of his men could ski well, which would help them move quickly over the snow of Antarctica. Also, Captain Scott was going to use ponies to drag his sleds, while Amundsen was using sled dogs, which were more used to the weather in Antarctica and could travel over the ice sheets and mountains of Antarctica more easily than ponies.

On October 19, 1911, Amundsen and four of his men left their camp at the Bay of Whales and set off into the frozen lands of Antarctica. Amundsen crossed the Transantarctic Mountains by traveling over the Axel Heiberg **Glacier**, which was steep and covered in deep snow. Meanwhile, on November 1, Captain Scott and part of his expedition set out from Cape Evans and made their way to the Transantarctic Mountains. (The rest of the men on the expedition stayed behind in Cape Evans and waited for them to return.) Captain Scott's plan was to travel over the mountains through the Beardmore Glacier, which was less dangerous than the way Amundsen had taken, but also much longer.

Near the end of November, Amundsen's expedition was journeying through a place called the "Devil's Glacier," where there were many deep holes in the ice called crevasses. On December 14, 1911, they made it to the point at the very bottom of planet Earth, and Roald Amundsen became the first person to reach the South Pole. He placed the flag of Norway on the Pole and also left a note for Captain Scott. A few days later, Amundsen's expedition started back toward their camp on the Bay of Whales, which they reached on January 25, 1912.

While Amundsen and his men were at the South Pole, Captain Scott's expedition was still traveling across the Beardmore Glacier. Sadly, they had killed their ponies for food and also because Captain Scott did not think the ponies would be able to make it up the glacier. Because of this, his men had to drag their sleds themselves, and they were getting very tired. After almost three hard months, on January 17, 1912, Captain Scott and four of his men reached the South Pole, only to find the flag of Norway and Amundsen's note saying that he and his men had made it there first. Captain Scott and his men then turned around to go back to their camp at Cape Evans, knowing that all their hard work and suffering had been for nothing.

Things got worse for them along the way when the temperature dropped much lower than normal at that time of year in Antarctica. They got **frostbite**, and after weeks of freezing temperatures, two of Captain Scott's men died from the cold. He and his other two men tried to continue to Cape Evans, but in mid-March, they got trapped in a blizzard and were not able to walk because the wind was blowing so hard and knocking them over. They waited in a tent for almost ten days, getting weaker and weaker, and around March 29, Captain Scott and his men died.

Roald Amundsen and Robert Falcon Scott's race to the South Pole was one of the greatest adventures of all time. Captain Scott became known as a hero throughout Great Britain because of his death in Antarctica, and Amundsen continued to explore and take expeditions to the Arctic. Sadly, he disappeared while flying over the Atlantic Ocean in 1928.

Amundsen's expedition during their journey to the South Pole

Captain Scott's expedition at the South Pole
(Captain Scott is standing in the center)

Cross on top of Observation Hill in Antarctica, which was built in honor of Captain Scott by the men on his expedition who stayed behind in Cape Evans

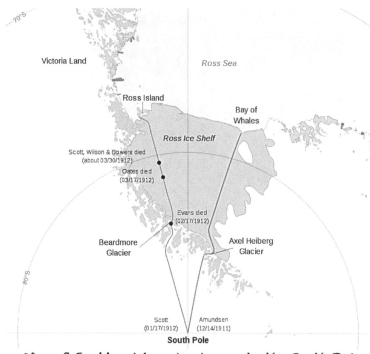

Map of Scott and Amundsen's race to the South Pole

REVIEW BITES

VOCABULARY

Telegram – a message that is sent using a machine called the telegraph

Advantages – things that help a person to accomplish something faster and more easily than someone else

Glacier – a large chunk of ice that forms near mountains

Frostbite – when a person loses feeling in their hands, feet, and face, and their skin changes color because of very cold temperatures

FUN FACT

One time, while he was on an expedition in northern Russia in 1918, Roald Amundsen was attacked by a polar bear. Thankfully, he was not seriously hurt because one of his dogs barked and charged at the polar bear, which made it run away.

REVIEW QUESTIONS

1. What country was Roald Amundsen from?

2. Which expedition won the race to the South Pole?

3. Why were Captain Robert Falcon Scott and his men not able to make it back to Cape Evans?

President Theodore Roosevelt (right) in a canoe on the River of Doubt

The Amazon River in South America is one of the longest rivers in the world. It is surrounded by the Amazon Rainforest, which is home to many dangerous animals, such as anaconda snakes, alligators, and piranhas. (Piranhas are fish that eat other fish, large animals, and people.) There are many rivers in South America that are **tributaries** of the Amazon River, including the Aripuanã River in Brazil.

Theodore Roosevelt was the 26th president of the United States, and he was a very adventurous man. Throughout his life, he traveled to many places in the United States, Europe, and Africa. After serving as president from 1901-1909, he was invited by the government of Argentina in South America to visit their country.

His son Kermit was living in Brazil at that time, and President Roosevelt decided to accept the government's invitation so he could see different parts of South America and also visit his son.

In October of 1913, President Roosevelt sailed from New York City to South America, and for two months, he spent time in Brazil, Uruguay, Argentina, and Chile. During this time, Lauro Müller, who worked for the government of Brazil, told President Roosevelt about the River of Doubt, which is a tributary of the Aripuanã River and the only river in South America that had not been explored at the time. No one knew how long the river was, nor what dangers a person might face if they sailed on it. President Roosevelt was excited about the idea of exploring it, and in December of 1913, after finishing his tour of South America, he began the long journey to the River of Doubt through the deserts and jungles of Paraguay and Brazil. His son Kermit decided to join him on the expedition, along with a man named Colonel Cândido Rondon, who was a famous soldier and explorer from Brazil. Colonel Rondon knew a lot about the lands around the Amazon River and the native people who lived there.

In February of 1914, President Roosevelt's expedition reached the River of Doubt, and on February 27, he and twenty-one men set off in canoes down the river and began their voyage. It was rainy in Brazil at that time, and because of this, the water was higher than normal and moved quickly. The days were hot, and insects like mosquitoes were always buzzing around (and biting) President Roosevelt and his men.

Over the next few weeks, President Roosevelt's expedition made their way down the river, but many times, they had to pull the heavy canoes out of the water and drag them through the rainforest because they could not sail through the river's rapids. They also had to be careful not to stand in the water for too long because they did not want to be eaten by piranhas. One time, President Roosevelt got bit in the foot by a poisonous coral snake, but thankfully, the snake's teeth did not touch his skin because of the thick boots he was wearing.

On March 15, the expedition was continuing down the river when one of the canoes was sucked into a whirlpool and pushed over a waterfall. Sadly, one of the men in the canoe disappeared into the water and died. Around one week later, President Roosevelt cut his leg on a rock in the river and got an **infection** that made him very sick.

At this same time, the expedition was running out of food, and on April 3, things went from bad to worse when one of the men named Julio killed another man named Paishon, who had caught Julio trying to steal food. After he killed Paishon, Julio ran away into the rainforest to hide, and he was never seen again.

President Roosevelt and his men were starting to worry that they would not make it to the end of the river alive. At night, they could hear people moving around in the rainforest near their camp. These were native people known as the Cinta Larga, who used poisoned arrows to kill their enemies. They followed President Roosevelt and his men the entire way down the river.

On April 26, the expedition reached the end of the River of Doubt. They had traveled almost five hundred miles, and by the end of the journey, President Roosevelt was so weak from his infection that he could barely sit up in his canoe. Over the next few months, he slowly began to recover, and he eventually gave speeches around the United

States about his expedition, which was one of the greatest adventures in history. Theodore Roosevelt died just a few years later in 1919, and the River of Doubt was renamed the Roosevelt River in his honor. (You can learn more about Theodore Roosevelt in my books *U.S. Presidential History Bites* and *In/Famous People History Bites Volume 2*.)

President Roosevelt (right, holding white mug) with members of his expedition

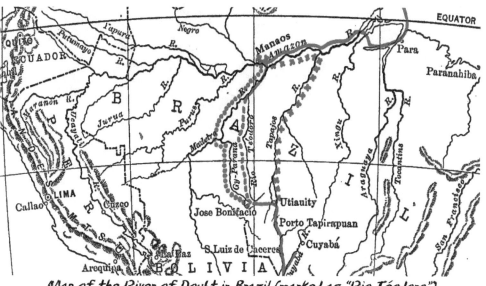

Map of the River of Doubt in Brazil (marked as "Rio Téodoro")

REVIEW BITES

VOCABULARY

Tributaries – small rivers that flow into larger rivers

Infection – when germs get into a person's body and cause them to become sick

FUN FACT

Theodore Roosevelt liked to try new things and take chances in his life. Because of this, his wife Edith asked their son Kermit to keep an eye on his father during the River of Doubt expedition to make sure he did not do anything crazy and that he came home alive.

REVIEW QUESTIONS

1. What continent is the River of Doubt located in?

2. What is the name of the fish in the River of Doubt that eat other fish, large animals, and people?

3. Why was Theodore Roosevelt so weak near the end of his expedition?

1. South America 2. Piranhas 3. He had cut his leg on a rock in the River of Doubt and gotten an infection that made him very sick

Ernest Shackleton's Antarctic Expedition 1914–1916

Ernest Shackleton

Shackleton (right) and his friend
Frank Hurley in Antarctica in 1915

Ernest Shackleton was born in 1874 in Ireland. When he grew up, he joined the British Royal Navy and served under Captain Robert Falcon Scott, who later led the British expedition to the South Pole (see Chapter 16: "Scott and Amundsen's Race to the South Pole"). While he was in the navy, Shackleton spent two years in Antarctica and decided that he wanted to explore it more. Between 1907–1909, he led an expedition to Antarctica to try to reach the South Pole, but he and his men had to turn around before reaching it because they were running out of food.

After Roald Amundsen became the first person to make it to the South Pole, Shackleton decided to lead an expedition to try to make the first journey across Antarctica from the Weddell Sea to the Ross Sea. He bought a ship called the *Endurance*, which had been built to break through ice in the water around Antarctica. In August of 1914, Shackleton and his crew left Great Britain and traveled to the island of South Georgia in the Atlantic Ocean, which was the last **inhabited** place before reaching Antarctica. On November 5, they arrived at the island and spent a few weeks there preparing for their journey.

In early December, Shackleton and twenty-seven men left South Georgia and set sail on the *Endurance* towards Antarctica. They had sled dogs on board, along with plenty of food and supplies for the expedition. As they traveled south, the temperature got much colder, and they began to see a lot of ice in the water. Eventually, they reached the Weddell Sea off the coast of Antarctica, and it was covered in ice **floes**.

For weeks, the *Endurance* pushed through the floes, but on January 18, 1915, the ship became trapped in the ice and could not move. Shackleton and his men were stuck in the coldest area of the world and were hundreds of miles from anyone who could help. Even when things were very difficult, though, Shackleton was known for persevering and trying to solve problems. His men called him "the Boss," not because he was mean, but because they looked up to him and trusted him to lead them.

Shackleton's expedition had no choice but to stay on the *Endurance* and wait for the ice around it to melt so they could start sailing again. Weeks turned into months, and still the ship did not move. Shackleton and his men sometimes tried to free it by using tools like ice axes, but they were unsuccessful. They tried to stay busy by cleaning the ship, playing soccer in the snow, and writing in their **journals**. Thankfully, they had plenty of food and water that they had packed for their trip across Antarctica.

In October of 1915, after being stuck for ten months, the ice around the *Endurance* began to close tighter around the ship and crush it. On October 27, Shackleton ordered his men to abandon (leave) the ship. (Eventually, in November, the *Endurance* sank completely under the water.) They set up camp on an ice floe and began to plan a journey north to a group of islands off the coast of Antarctica. Traveling across the ice was very difficult because they were pulling a lot of weight on their sleds, including three small lifeboats from the *Endurance*, which they hoped to use if they made it to open water. Shackleton's expedition spent more than four months on ice floes, trying to get farther north. They hunted seals and penguins for extra food, and sometimes, giant killer whales swam very close to the floes they were on.

On April 9, 1916, the ice underneath Shackleton and his men began to melt, and they were able to get into their lifeboats and sail through the now-open water. A few days later, they reached Elephant Island off the coast of Antarctica, but they were still a long way from safety on South Georgia Island. Shackleton knew that his men would eventually die if they did not get help. So, on April 24, Shackleton and five of his men set out from Elephant Island in one of the lifeboats (called the *James Caird*) to try to reach South Georgia, which was around eight hundred miles away. The area of ocean that Shackleton and his men had to cross was the most dangerous in the world. The weather was very cold and stormy, and during the journey, their small boat crashed over huge waves.

Amazingly, though, after two weeks of sailing, they saw South Georgia in the distance. On May 10, they landed at King Haakon Bay, but the problem was that the only people who lived on the island in a town called Stromness were on the other side of the island. In between the men and Stromness were glaciers with crevasses (deep holes) and tall, icy mountains which no one had ever climbed before. Even though he was very tired, Shackleton was determined to save his men back on Elephant Island. Over the next several days, he crossed the dangerous island, and on May 20, he reached Stromness. By that time, he had grown such a thick beard and looked so weak that the people there did not recognize him.

Shackleton got another ship and sailed south back towards Elephant Island. He tried to reach it three times, but ice blocked his way. Finally, during his fourth try, on August 30, 1916, Shackleton reached the island and found all of his men still alive and waiting for him. They all boarded (got on) the ship, and after nearly two long years in Antarctica, they were finally going home.

Ernest Shackleton became known around the world for his Antarctic expedition, which was one of the greatest adventures of all time. He gave many speeches and wrote a book about it before he died in 1922.

The Endurance trapped in ice
on the Weddell Sea in 1915

Sled dogs watching the Endurance
being destroyed by ice chunks

Shackleton's expedition pushing the James Caird
lifeboat into the water off of Elephant Island

Island of South Georgia, which Shackleton and his men crossed

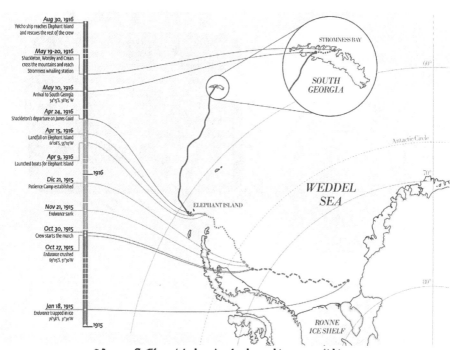

Map of Shackleton's Antarctic expedition
© Luca Ferrario, DensityDesign Research Lab (refer to page 207)

REVIEW BITES

VOCABULARY

Inhabited – lived in/on by people

Floes – large chunks of ice that float on top of water

Journals – notebooks that people write in to keep track of things they do

Determined – when a person does not give up and tries hard to accomplish something

FUN FACT

During their journey across South Georgia, Ernest Shackleton and his men reached the top of a mountain and saw that the other side was covered in snow. In order to save time, Shackleton said that they should slide down the mountain, and so, he and his men sat down and slid hundreds of feet in the snow. They made it to the bottom without getting hurt and then continued on their journey.

REVIEW QUESTIONS

1. What was the name of
Ernest Shackleton's ship?

2. What body of water did the
Endurance get trapped in?

3. How many miles of water did Shackleton
and his men have to cross in the *James
Caird* lifeboat to reach South Georgia?

Lindbergh's Flight Across the Atlantic
1927

Charles Lindbergh in front of the Spirit of St. Louis

The first airplane was invented in 1903 by two brothers named Orville and Wilbur Wright, who were from Dayton, Ohio. It looked very different from airplanes today, and in the early 1900s, many airplanes were **unstable** and not safe to fly in. During World War I, the United States and other countries used airplanes to discover where enemies were located and how many soldiers and weapons they had.

In 1919, one year after World War I ended, a **businessman** from New York City named Raymond Orteig announced that he would give a $25,000 prize to the first person to fly across the Atlantic Ocean from New York City to Paris, France ($25,000 at that time

113

was equal to about $400,000 today). One pilot who wanted to win Orteig's prize was a young man named Charles Lindbergh.

Charles Lindbergh was born in 1902 in Detroit, Michigan, and when he was a boy, he became very interested in mechanics, which is the study of how machines work. In 1922, he went to the Nebraska Aircraft Corporation to learn how to fly airplanes, and he became a very good pilot. A few years later, he began delivering the mail in an airplane between the cities of St. Louis, Missouri, and Chicago, Illinois. This was a very dangerous job because the pilots had to fly through stormy weather, and many of them died. Lindbergh loved to fly, though, and in 1926, he decided to try to win Orteig's prize and fly across the Atlantic Ocean from New York City to Paris, France.

Unlike other pilots who wanted to win the prize, he decided to go alone so that his plane would weigh less and be able to fly faster. People thought that Lindbergh was crazy because they did not think that he would be able to stay awake for the whole flight, which could take almost two days. (Other people had already flown over the Atlantic Ocean, but not between New York City and Paris, and no one had ever flown alone.)

Several businessmen from St. Louis, Missouri, decided to help Lindbergh and bought him a plane, which Lindbergh named the *Spirit of St. Louis*. By May of 1927, he was ready to make his flight, and people around the United States became very excited to see if he would succeed. (That same month, two pilots from France disappeared over the Atlantic Ocean while trying to win Orteig's prize.) At 7:52 a.m. on May 20, 1927, Charles Lindbergh took off in the *Spirit of St. Louis* on the runway at Roosevelt Field in New York City. He flew north over the countryside of eastern Canada, and around 8:00 p.m. that night, he started flying over the Atlantic Ocean. Fog (low clouds) formed over the water, and it became very dark. Soon after, Lindbergh saw a storm cloud ahead and tried to pass through it. However, the temperature was so low that the water inside the cloud began turning into ice on his plane, and he had to turn back and fly around the big cloud instead.

As Lindbergh continued flying, he began to feel very tired. He knew that if he fell asleep, he would lose control of the plane and crash. He tried hard to keep himself awake. Sometimes, he flew very low and close to the ocean so that he would have to fly over the waves and pay close attention. He also opened the windows of his plane to let cold air blow in to make him feel less tired.

Early in the morning on May 21, 1927, the sun came up over the horizon, and Lindbergh continued toward Paris. Several hours later, he looked down and saw fishing boats below on the water, and he knew that he was getting close to land. At 3:00 p.m. in the afternoon, he reached the western coast of Ireland, which is a country close to Great Britain. From there, he flew over Britain and then the English Channel. By the time Lindbergh made it to France, it was nighttime again, and he could see the lights of the city of Paris in the distance. While going over Paris, he flew around the Eiffel Tower, which is a famous landmark in that city.

At 10:22 p.m. on May 21, Lindbergh landed the *Spirit of St. Louis* at Le Bourget Airport in Paris and became the first person to fly solo (alone) across the Atlantic Ocean. When he landed, a crowd of over 100,000 very excited people surrounded his plane, pulled him out of it, and carried him on their shoulders. People all over the world heard about his flight across the Atlantic, which was one of the greatest adventures in history. Charles Lindbergh became very well known and received awards like the Legion of Honor from France and the Medal of Honor from the United States. He lived for many more years and died in 1974 in Hawaii.

Storm over the Atlantic Ocean

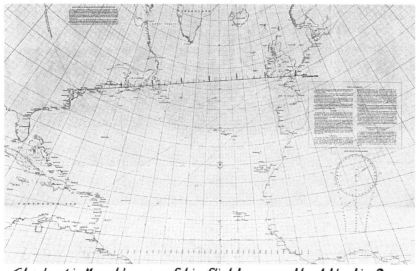

Charles Lindbergh's map of his flight across the Atlantic Ocean

REVIEW BITES

VOCABULARY

Unstable – when something is not strong or steady

Businessman – a man who owns a company that sells things to people

Runway – a long, smooth area of ground at an airport that planes take off from and land on

Horizon – the line in the distance where the sky and ground meet

FUN FACT

In June of 1927, after Charles Lindbergh returned to the United States, a parade was held for him in New York City. Over four million people came to see him as he rode in a car through the streets of the city.

REVIEW QUESTIONS

1. What did someone have to do to win Raymond Orteig's prize of $25,000?

2. What was the name of Charles Lindbergh's plane?

3. What did Lindbergh do to stay awake during his flight across the Atlantic Ocean?

1. Fly across the Atlantic Ocean from New York City to Paris, France 2. *Spirit of St. Louis* 3. Sometimes, he flew very low and close to the ocean so that he would have to fly over the waves and pay close attention. He also opened the windows of his plane to let cold air blow in to make him feel less tired.

Maurice Wilson's Extraordinary Journey
1933-1934

Maurice Wilson in front of his plane Ever-Wrest

Mt. Everest is the tallest mountain in the world at 29,032 feet high, and it is located on the border of China and Nepal. It is very difficult and dangerous to climb Mt. Everest because the weather is cold and snowy, and there are many places to slip and fall thousands of feet down the mountain. There is also very little **oxygen** in the air. In 1922, mountain climbers from Great Britain became the first people to try to climb to the top of Mt. Everest, but they never made it because an avalanche (huge pile of falling snow and ice) killed seven of the men who were carrying supplies for the expedition. Over the next several years, other expeditions tried to reach the top of the mountain, but they all did not make it.

Then, during the early 1930s, an **eccentric** businessman from Great Britain named Maurice Wilson decided that he was going to fly to Nepal, land his plane on the lower parts of Mt. Everest, and climb the rest of the way to the top. There were two problems with his plan: one, he had never climbed a mountain before, and two, he barely knew how to fly an airplane. Also, the governments of India and Nepal had not given him permission to fly over their countries. However, Wilson was determined, and on May 21, 1933, he waved goodbye to his friends and took off from London, England, in his plane, which he had named *Ever-Wrest* as a play on the word "Everest." After flying south over Europe and the Mediterranean Sea, he reached the hot, desert lands of North Africa and continued on to the Middle East.

Wilson stopped to put fuel in his plane in Bahrain, which is an island in the Middle East that was ruled by Great Britain at that time. A worker for the British government in Bahrain named Colonel Percy Loch ordered Wilson to not continue to Mt. Everest because he had not received permission to fly in India or Nepal. Wilson told the colonel he would return home to Great Britain, and on the morning of June 1, he took off in his plane and left Bahrain. However, he tricked Colonel Loch and headed across the Persian Gulf toward India instead. Wilson flew around seven hundred miles that day, and his plane was almost out of fuel by the time he landed in the city of Gwadar on the western coast of India.

After Wilson arrived in India, workers of the British government there took his plane away from him and would not let him fly any farther. This did not stop him from trying to climb Mt. Everest, though. For the next several months, he lived in the city of Darjeeling, India, and began secretly making plans for the next part of his journey. Wilson hired three Sherpas (native people of Nepal) to travel with him, and early in the morning on March 20, 1934, he left Darjeeling disguised as a Chinese **priest** so that workers of the British government would not recognize him. Together, Wilson and the three Sherpas walked hundreds of miles through the regions of Sikkim (in India) and Tibet (in China) to reach Mt. Everest.

As they got closer to the mountain, the weather became cold and snowy, and on April 14, 1934, they arrived in the Rongbuk Valley near the base of Everest. Wilson tried to make it to the top, but it was hard for him to breathe and stay warm. Also, because he did not know how to climb mountains, he had not brought the right boots and tools to climb over the ice and rocks. On May 29, while he and the Sherpas were at their camp at 21,000 feet, Wilson set off alone to try to climb the rest of the way to the top. By this time, though, he was very cold and weak, and he never came back to the camp where the Sherpas were waiting for him. One year later, British climbers found Wilson's frozen dead body on the mountain at around 23,000 feet high.

Maurice Wilson's **extraordinary** journey was one of the greatest adventures of all time, and it inspired other climbers to try to reach the top of Mt. Everest.

Bahrain during the mid-1900s

Rongbuk Valley in front of Mt. Everest

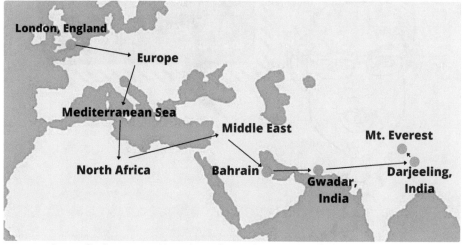

Map of Maurice Wilson's extraordinary journey by L.B. Dugan

VOCABULARY

Oxygen – a gas in the air that people need to breathe in order to stay alive

Eccentric – unique in a strange way

Priest – a person who offers sacrifices to God or gods as part of their religion

Extraordinary – unusual and amazing

FUN FACT

Before 1933, Maurice Wilson lived and worked in Great Britain, the United States, and New Zealand. He first got the idea to climb Mt. Everest while he was on vacation in Germany and read a story about the mountain in a newspaper.

REVIEW QUESTIONS

1. What country was Maurice Wilson from?

2. How did Wilson make it out of the city of Darjeeling, India?

3. Did Maurice Wilson reach the top of Mt. Everest?

1. Great Britain 2. He disguised himself as a Chinese priest so that workers of the British government would not recognize him 3. No

Amelia Earhart

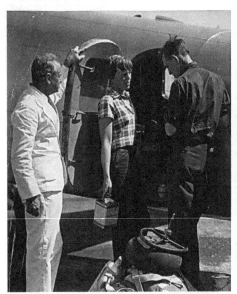

*Earhart (center) and Fred Noonan
(right) in Port Darwin, Australia*

Amelia Earhart was born in 1897 in Atchison, Kansas. When she was twenty-three years old, she went on her first airplane ride and loved it so much that she decided to become a pilot. In 1923, she earned her pilot's **license** and began to look for ways to set records that no female pilot had ever set before. In 1932, five years after Charles Lindbergh's famous flight, Earhart became the first woman to fly solo (alone) across the Atlantic Ocean, and she received an award called the Distinguished Flying Cross. In 1935, she became the first person to fly solo from Honolulu, Hawaii, to Oakland, California. Her accomplishments made her famous in the United States, and she inspired many women across the country.

Earhart wanted to become the first woman to fly around the world (an American man named Wiley Post had been the first person to do it in 1931). Her plan was to fly with a **navigator** named Fred Noonan from Miami, Florida, around the world to Oakland, California. The type of plane she was going to fly was called a Lockheed Electra. On the morning of June 1, 1937, Earhart and Noonan took off from the Miami airport and began their journey. They flew over the Bahamas and Puerto Rico, and on June 2, they landed in the city of Caripito, Venezuela, in South America. Over the next few days, they flew over the jungles of South America and the Amazon River. On June 6, Earhart and Noonan landed in Natal, Brazil, where they planned to start their flight across the Atlantic Ocean between South America and Africa.

Early the next morning, Earhart and Noonan left Brazil and had to fly through rain over the Atlantic Ocean. After more than thirteen hours of flying, they reached St. Louis in Senegal, Africa. Soon after that, Earhart and Noonan flew to the city of Dakar in Senegal, which was ruled by France at that time. While in Dakar, Earhart met with important leaders of the French government in a t-shirt and pants because she had packed very few clothes so her plane would fly faster and use less fuel.

Over the next several days, Earhart and Noonan flew across Central Africa and had to avoid sandstorms and tornadoes. On June 13, they landed in the city of Massawa, which is next to the Red Sea in the country of Eritrea and is one of the hottest cities in the world. There they refueled their plane and made sure that everything was working correctly. On June 15, Earhart and Noonan took off and flew over the Middle East. That night, they landed in India, where they spent time sightseeing and going on camel rides.

On June 18, while flying over Southeast Asia, they flew into a storm, and the rain was so hard that it took some of the paint off of their plane. Earhart and Noonan made it through the storm and stopped in the countries of Myanmar and Thailand before heading south towards Australia. Along the way, they landed on the beautiful island of Java, where the ocean water was **turquoise** and the land was made up of green mountains and volcanoes. They really enjoyed their time on the island and spent several days driving around and hiking. On June 27, they left Java, and one day later, they reached Port Darwin on the northern coast of Australia.

From there, Earhart and Noonan flew to the island of New Guinea, where they began to prepare for their long flight across the Pacific Ocean. Their plan was to first fly to the tiny Howland Island in the middle of the ocean and then continue from there. The *Itasca* ship from the United States Navy was near Howland Island and stayed in radio contact with Earhart in order to help her navigate to the island.

At 10:00 a.m. on July 2, 1937, Earhart and Noonan took off from New Guinea and headed toward Howland Island. Several hours later, while flying over the Pacific Ocean, Earhart told the sailors on the *Itasca* ship that her plane was running out of fuel. The *Itasca* did not receive any more radio messages from Earhart after that. She and Fred Noonan disappeared and were never found. No one knows what happened to them.

Amelia Earhart became even more well known because of her **mysterious** disappearance, and her final flight was one of the greatest adventures in history. (You can learn more about her in my book *In/Famous People History Bites Volume 2*.)

Island of Java

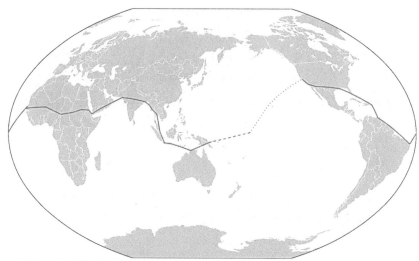
Map of Amelia Earhart's final flight (the dotted line shows the portion of her journey that she did not complete) © Hellerick (refer to page 207)

REVIEW BITES

VOCABULARY

License – a government document that a person needs in order to do things like drive a car or fly an airplane

Navigator – someone who uses maps to figure out which way to go during a trip

Turquoise – a bright bluish-green color

Mysterious – cannot be explained

FUN FACT

Amelia Earhart was friends with First Lady Eleanor Roosevelt, who was the wife of U.S. President Franklin D. Roosevelt. Earhart helped to teach Mrs. Roosevelt how to fly, and the First Lady eventually earned a student's pilot license.

REVIEW QUESTIONS

1. Who was the first woman to fly solo across the Atlantic Ocean?

2. What was the name of the beautiful island where Amelia Earhart and Fred Noonan stopped during their flight around the world?

3. What happened to Earhart and Noonan while they were flying to Howland Island?

Slavomir Rawicz's Journey to India 1941-1942

Gobi Desert in Mongolia

Slavomir Rawicz was born in 1915 in Poland, which is a country in Europe that is next to Germany and Ukraine. His mother was from Russia, and she taught her son to speak Russian. When he grew up, Rawicz joined the Polish **cavalry**, and in 1939, he fought to defend his country when Germany and Russia attacked Poland during World War II. (You can learn more about World War II in my book *Major Wars History Bites.*) Poland was taken over by Germany and Russia, and in November of 1939, the Russians arrested Rawicz because he spoke Russian and they thought that he might be working as a spy for the Polish government.

After spending a year in prison, Rawicz was sent to a labor (work) camp in Siberia, which is an area of land in Russia and one of the coldest places in the world. In February of 1941, Rawicz and five thousand other prisoners arrived at the camp and were forced to do hard work in freezing weather. Eventually, he and six other prisoners decided to try to escape from the camp and walk to freedom in India, which was ruled by Great Britain at that time and was about four thousand miles away.

So, one night in April of 1941, while the rest of the prisoners were sleeping, Rawicz and six **companions** crawled through a hole in the bottom of the fence around the camp and escaped. There was a snowstorm that night, and because of this, the Russian guards at the camp could not see the men while they escaped.

Rawicz and his companions began walking south and crossed the Lena River, which was very cold. They continued on, and near the northern part of Lake Baikal (the largest lake in Siberia), they encountered a young Polish girl named Kristina, who had also escaped from a work camp in Siberia. Kristina joined the group, and in June, the eight of them crossed into the country of Mongolia. Soon after, they entered the Gobi Desert, which is one of the hottest deserts in the world. There were many days that they could not find any water to drink.

In August, while they were crossing the desert, Kristina and one of the men named Sigmund Makowski died from **exhaustion**, and Rawicz and his companions were very sad. In order to survive, they killed and ate desert snakes, and after a few more difficult weeks, they finally made it to the end of the Gobi Desert and walked into the region of Gansu in China.

While they were journeying through China, they were able to stay at the houses of **hospitable** Chinese people who lived in the countryside. The men asked for directions to Lhasa, which was a famous city in the region of Tibet in China and close to India. In November, they made it to Lake Namtso near Lhasa, but they decided to not go into the city because they were afraid that government workers in Lhasa would not be friendly to them. Around this time, one of the men named Zacharius Marchinkovas died from exhaustion. The rest of the men continued on toward the Himalayan Mountains on the border of China and India, which are the highest mountains in the world.

Over the next three months, the weather got snowy and much colder, and in March of 1942, Rawicz and his companions began crossing over the icy Himalayas. They tried to spend their nights in caves whenever they could find them in order to escape the cold. One day, while they were climbing down a mountain, one of the men named Anton Paluchowicz fell into a deep crevasse (hole) and disappeared. Rawicz and the other three men were sad and discouraged, but they continued on. In April, they made it through the Himalayas and at last reached India after walking four thousand miles from Siberia. While in India, Rawicz and his three companions met a group of British soldiers, who took them to Calcutta, India. Rawicz spent a month in a hospital there because he was so weak from his journey. He eventually moved to Great Britain, where he lived until his death in 2004.

Slavomir Rawicz's journey to India was one of the greatest adventures of all time, and he wrote a book about it called *The Long Walk*, which has been translated into over twenty languages.

Lake Namtso in Tibet © Reurinkjan (refer to page 207)

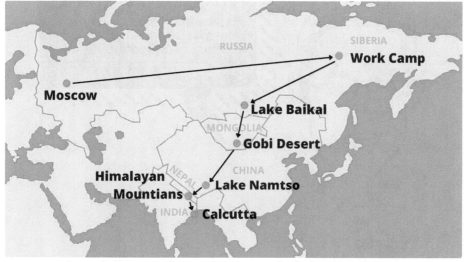

Map of Slavomir Rawicz's journey to India *by L.B. Dugan*

REVIEW BITES

VOCABULARY

Cavalry – the part of the military in which soldiers ride on horses

Companions – friends on a journey

Exhaustion – when a person is very tired and his/her body becomes extremely weak

Hospitable – when someone is friendly to strangers and is willing to share their home and food with others

FUN FACT

In his book *The Long Walk*, Slavomir Rawicz wrote that while he and his companions were crossing the Himalayan Mountains, they saw two tall animals that looked like Abominable Snowmen, which are big, scary creatures that some people believe live in the Himalayas.

REVIEW QUESTIONS

1. Why was Slavomir Rawicz arrested by the Russians?

2. What was the name of the desert that Rawicz and his companions crossed?

3. How many miles did Rawicz and his companions walk from Siberia to India?

1. Because he spoke Russian, and the Russians thought that he might be working as a spy for the Polish government 2. Gobi Desert 3. Four thousand

136

Damon Gause's Escape to Australia
1942

Drawing of Damon Gause, one of the planes he flew, and the Ruth-Lee boat

Jungle in the Philippines

Damon Gause was born in 1915 in Georgia, and as a young man, he loved to spend time hunting and boxing. In 1941, he joined the United States Army Air Corps, which later became the U.S. Air Force. In November of that same year, Gause was sent to a group of islands in the Pacific Ocean called the Philippines to fly airplanes in the 27th Bombardment Group. At that time, World War II was being fought between the Axis and the Allies, and on December 7, 1941, Japan attacked the United States at Pearl Harbor, Hawaii. Because of this attack, the United States entered World War II and began fighting against Japan in the Pacific Ocean. (You can learn more about World War II in my book *Major Wars History Bites.*)

Unfortunately for Gause and his fellow soldiers, Japan began an attack on the Philippines using planes, ships, and soldiers. The Japanese terrorized the Philippine people (called Filipinos) and surrounded Gause and the Americans in the region of Bataan. On April 9, 1942, the Americans in Bataan surrendered to the Japanese and were taken prisoner by them. Soon after this, Gause escaped from the prison camp where he and the other soldiers were being held, and he decided to try to reach Australia, which had not been captured by the Japanese. At this same time, the Japanese were conquering other islands in the Pacific Ocean and were also bombing Australia. Gause's trip would be dangerous because many places along the way were controlled by the Japanese, but he was determined to get back home to his wife, Ruth.

One of Gauses's friends in the Philippines was a young woman named Rita Garcia, and she also wanted to escape from the Philippines. Near the end of May of 1942, she and Gause walked through the jungles of the Philippines to Balayan Bay, and from there, they sailed in a small boat to the island of Lubang. They spent several weeks on the island living with the Filipinos there, who hated the Japanese and loved the Americans.

Gause began to plan the next part of his journey with an American soldier named William Osborne, who had also escaped from Bataan. Together, they set sail from Lubang Island in a 20-foot-long motorboat that they named the *Ruth-Lee* after their wives, Ruth and Lee. Gause made the hard decision to leave his friend Rita behind with the Filipinos because he knew their voyage would be very dangerous. He and Osborne brought a Japanese flag with them to put on the **mast** of their boat in case they sailed near Japanese ships. In mid-August, they sailed to the island of Mindoro and then went on to Culion Island, where they made **repairs** to the motor on their boat.

From there, Gause and Osborne continued south toward Australia, and on September 1, they reached Brooke's Point on Palawan Island. The Filipinos there said that they should wait to sail because a storm was coming. Gause and Osborne had been sailing in rough waters before, though, and they thought that this storm would not be much worse than what they had already encountered. They were wrong. They sailed into a typhoon, which is a huge storm over the ocean, and large waves crashed onto their boat. Gause and Osborne had to use buckets to throw water out of the boat so it would not sink. After a few days, the storm finally calmed down, and the two men sailed down the east coast of the island of Borneo through the Makassar Strait. While in this strait, they passed by Japanese warships and raised their Japanese flag so that the sailors would think they were on Japan's side.

At the beginning of October, Gause and Osborne reached the island of Timor, which was the last island between them and Australia. Over the next few days, they sailed in very hot weather, and their skin became cracked. Then, on October 4, the two men spotted the northern coast of Australia in the distance. After reaching land, they could not find any people and spent the next several days sailing toward the city of Wyndham. On October 11, Gause and Osborne encountered a group of Australian sailors, who gave them food and water. That same day, they reached Wyndham, Australia, and were safe at last after their voyage of 3,200 miles.

Gause and Osborne returned home to the United States and continued to fight for their country during World War II. William Osborne also served in the Korean and Vietnam Wars and died in 1985. Sadly, Damon Gause died in 1944 during World War II in a plane crash near London, England. His escape from the Philippines to Australia was one of the greatest adventures in history.

Makassar Strait © Marwan Mohamad (refer to page 208)

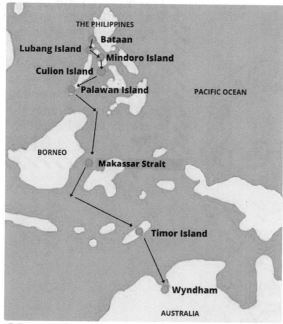

Map of Damon Gause's escape to Australia by L.B. Dugan

REVIEW BITES

VOCABULARY

Terrorized – scared people by hurting them and/or by destroying their home and belongings

Mast – a pole in the center of a boat that a sail is attached to so that wind can blow the boat forward

Repairs – fixes to a machine to make it work properly

FUN FACT

After they arrived in Australia, Damon Gause and William Osborne were brought to see U.S. General Douglas MacArthur, who was in the city of Brisbane, Australia, at that time. General MacArthur was amazed by their story and gave each of them an award called the Distinguished Service Cross.

REVIEW QUESTIONS

1. Where was Damon Gause sent to in November of 1941?

2. Whom did Gause escape to Australia with?

3. Why did Gause and Osborne take a Japanese flag with them on their voyage?

1. The Philippines 2. An American soldier named William Osborne 3. To put on the mast of their boat in case they sailed near any Japanese ships

Thor Heyerdahl with a statue
© Bjørn Fjørtoft (refer to page 208)

French Polynesia

French Polynesia is a group of over one hundred islands in the South Pacific Ocean that have been ruled by France since the mid-1800s. Some of the most famous islands in French Polynesia include Tahiti, Bora Bora, and the Society Islands. For many years, historians believed that French Polynesia was first settled by people from other islands in the Pacific Ocean, but a man named Thor Heyerdahl did not agree with this idea.

Thor Heyerdahl was born in 1914 in Norway, and as a boy, he became fascinated with the islands of the Pacific Ocean and wanted to become an explorer when he grew up. From 1933-1936, he attended the University of Oslo in Oslo, Norway, and studied **biology** and

geography. In 1936, he and his wife, Liv, traveled to French Polynesia and spent a year living there, learning about the history and culture of the region. During that time, Heyerdahl began to wonder if French Polynesia had actually first been settled by native people of South America. There was an old legend about a South American chief (leader) named Kon-Tiki. According to this legend, he had begun a voyage from Peru in South America in a raft made of balsa wood and sailed west on the Pacific Ocean, possibly reaching French Polynesia.

Over the next ten years, Heyerdahl continued studying and writing about French Polynesia, and in 1946, he talked with a group of American historians about whether or not they thought it would have been possible for South Americans to sail to French Polynesia many years ago. One of the historians, named Herbert Spinden, **sarcastically** said to Heyerdahl, "Sure, see how far you get yourself sailing from Peru to the South Pacific on a balsa raft!"

So, in early 1947, Heyerdahl planned an expedition to do just that: sail from Peru to French Polynesia to show that people from South America could have been the first settlers of French Polynesia. He got together a crew of five men named Knut, Bengt, Erik, Torstein, and Herman. Together, they went to South America and built a 45-foot-long raft out of balsa wood and named it the *Kon-Tiki.* The raft had a sail, but no motor because they wanted it to be similar to the rafts that they believed South Americans would have used hundreds of years earlier.

On April 28, 1947, Heyerdahl and his crew left the city of Callao, Peru, and set out on the Pacific Ocean on their small raft.

They brought food such as potatoes and coconuts to eat, but they also fished during their voyage and caught dolphins and even small sharks. A current called the Humboldt Current pushed them northwest toward the **equator**.

One day, near the end of May, they noticed a whale shark swimming underneath their raft. Whale sharks are the biggest fish in the world, and the men were worried that it would flip the *Kon-Tiki* over. After about an hour, the whale shark finally swam away, and Heyerdahl and his men continued traveling toward the equator. On June 10, the South Equatorial Current began moving their raft southwest in the direction of French Polynesia.

Heyerdahl was worried about the possibility of a wave flipping him and his men off their raft. Then, on July 2, they encountered a rogue wave, which is a big wave that is all by itself in the water. Thankfully, the *Kon-Tiki* sailed over it without any issues (problems), but a few weeks later, near the end of July, a storm formed over the ocean. It was so powerful that the wind ripped the sail of the raft and broke some of the ropes holding it together.

Even after this damage, though, the *Kon-Tiki* continued sailing. On August 7, 1947, it crashed onto a reef (group of rocks in the water) next to the island of Raroia in French Polynesia. After traveling 4,300 miles in 101 days, Heyerdahl and his crew had accomplished their goal and proved that people from South America could have been the first settlers of French Polynesia.

Thor Heyerdahl wrote a book and made a movie about the *Kon-Tiki* voyage, which was one of the greatest adventures of all time.

He continued to explore and took several more incredible voyages before he died in 2002 in Italy.

Kon-Tiki *sailing on the Pacific Ocean* © *Nasjonalbiblioteket (refer to page 208)*

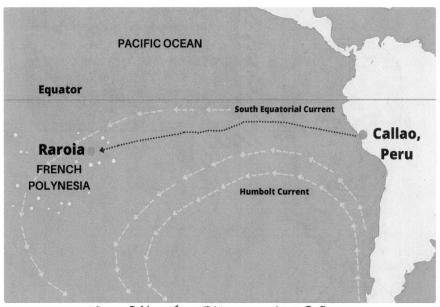

Map of the *Kon-Tiki* voyage *by L.B. Dugan*

REVIEW BITES

VOCABULARY

Biology – the study of how humans, plants, and animals live

Geography – the study of areas of land on the Earth

Sarcastically – when a person says something in a way that is meant to make fun of another person

Equator – a line drawn on world maps and globes that goes all the way around planet Earth and separates the northern part of the planet from the southern part

FUN FACT

During one night of their voyage on the *Kon-Tiki*, Thor Heyerdahl and his crew saw a fish called the snake mackerel, which jumped out of the water and onto their raft. Snake mackerels only hunt for food at night and are rarely (almost never) seen by humans.

REVIEW QUESTIONS

1. What did Thor Heyerdahl begin to wonder while he was living on the island of Fatu-Hiva?

2. What was the *Kon-Tiki?*

3. What kind of large fish swam underneath the *Kon-Tiki?*

1. Whether or not French Polynesia had actually first been settled by native people of South America 2. A 45-foot-long raft made out of balsa wood that Thor Heyerdahl and his crew used to cross the Pacific Ocean 3. Whale shark

Colonel Hunt's Everest Expedition
1953

Mt. Everest (Nepalese side of the mountain)

Mt. Everest is the tallest mountain in the world (29,032 feet) and is located in the Himalayan Mountains on the border of China and Nepal. Between 1922–1949, many expeditions from Great Britain traveled to China to climb Mt. Everest because the government of Nepal did not allow **foreigners** to enter the country and climb the mountain. None of these expeditions were able to climb to the top of Mt. Everest from the Chinese side. Then, in 1950, the government of Nepal decided to open the country to foreign climbers. Over the next two years, a few expeditions traveled to Mt. Everest through Nepal and began to figure out a way to climb the mountain from the Nepalese side.

In 1953, the Joint Himalayan **Committee** in Great Britain paid for a new Everest expedition to Nepal, and they chose a British soldier and climber named Colonel John Hunt to the be the leader of the expedition. Colonel Hunt got together a team of climbers from Great Britain and New Zealand, along with a group of Sherpas, who are native people of the area around Mt. Everest and are very good at climbing.

One of the climbers from New Zealand was Edmund Hillary, who had loved climbing mountains since he was young and had already been to Mt. Everest in 1951. The leader of the Sherpas was Tenzing Norgay, and he had been on several Everest expeditions. Hillary and Norgay quickly became friends.

In March of 1953, Colonel Hunt's expedition left Kathmandu, the capital city of Nepal, and began their long walk to reach Mt. Everest. They brought a lot of food and supplies, and along the way, they stopped in the towns of Namche Bazaar and Tengboche in the mountains, where the Sherpa people still live today. After a few weeks of walking, on April 12, the expedition reached Mt. Everest and set up a camp at a height of 17,900 feet. Mt. Everest is so big that climbers have to spend many days going up the mountain, and because of this, they set up other camps on the way to the top.

In mid-April, Colonel Hunt's expedition climbed through the Khumbu Icefall, which is a huge area of ice chunks and the most dangerous part of the mountain. The climbers had to walk on ladders over large crevasses and climb past tall ice towers that they hoped would not fall on them. They eventually made it through the Icefall, and near the end of April, they crossed a long glacier called the Western Cwm (pronounced "Koom").

The expedition had a difficult time climbing up the Lhotse Face, which is an enormous wall of ice and snow that goes almost straight up. Finally, on May 21, they reached the top of the Lhotse Face and were at an elevation (height) of around 25,000 feet. It was windy on the mountain, and it was hard for the climbers to breathe because there was very little oxygen in the air. They were able to get extra oxygen by carrying oxygen tanks on their backs and breathing through a face mask.

Colonel Hunt decided to send a team of two people up to reach the summit (top) of Mt. Everest because they could move faster than the whole group. On May 28, they set up a camp at 27,900 feet, from which Edmund Hillary and Tenzing Norgay would try to reach the top. Early the next day, on May 29, 1953, Hillary and Norgay set out from their camp and climbed slowly, step by step, toward the summit. At 9:30 a.m., they reached a point called the South Summit at 28,700 feet, and soon after, at 11:30 a.m., Hillary and Norgay made it to the summit and stood on top of the highest mountain on earth. They were very excited, and the news spread around the world that they had reached the top of Mt. Everest!

Colonel John Hunt's Everest Expedition was one of the greatest adventures of all time. Colonel Hunt and Edmund Hillary were knighted for their accomplishments (received the title "Sir" before their name), and Tenzing Norgay received an important award from Nepal called the Order of the Star of Nepal.

Edmund Hillary (left) and Tenzing Norgay © Jamling Norgay (refer to page 208)

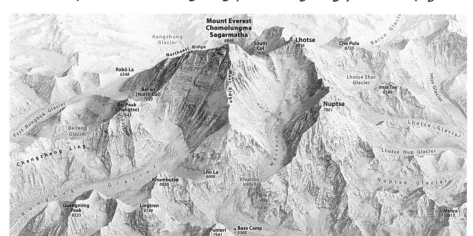

Map of Mt. Everest

From left to right: Saroj (Sherpa guide), Mike (Solomon's dad), Solomon, and Prem (Sherpa porter) on the Hillary Suspension Bridge (see "Fun Fact")

REVIEW BITES

VOCABULARY

Foreigners - people from a different country

Committee - a group of people who make decisions for a business, project, or expedition

FUN FACT

In the years after he climbed Mt. Everest, Sir Edmund Hillary spent a lot of time in Nepal helping the Sherpa people by building schools and hospitals in their towns. The Hillary Suspension Bridge near the Sherpa town of Namche Bazaar is named after him.

153

REVIEW QUESTIONS

1. Who are the native people of the area around Mt. Everest?

2. What is the most dangerous part of Mt. Everest?

3. Who were the first people to climb to the top of Mt. Everest?

1. Sherpas 2. Khumbu Icefall
3. Edmund Hillary and Tenzing Norgay

Voyage of the *Nautilus* Submarine 1958

The Nautilus *submarine in 1955*

The Space Race (1957-1969) was a time period in which the United States and Russia tried to beat each other to accomplish things in outer space. Russia started the race in October of 1957 when they launched the first **satellite** (called *Sputnik I*) into space. The United States tried to launch their own satellite in December of 1957, but it crashed and exploded soon after it took off.

The U.S. government wanted to accomplish something important so the United States would look like the strongest country in the world. They were also trying to figure out ways to have an advantage over Russia in case a war started between the two countries. At that time, the United States was building **submarines** that used nuclear power. Nuclear-powered submarines are fast, quiet, and able to stay underwater for a very long time. The first nuclear submarine was the USS *Nautilus*, which was built from 1952–1954. It was 320 feet long and could dive seven hundred feet underwater.

Near the end of 1957, the commander of the *Nautilus*, William R. Anderson, met with U.S. President Dwight D. Eisenhower and discussed the idea of the *Nautilus* sailing from the Pacific Ocean to the Atlantic Ocean by going underneath the North Pole. President Eisenhower liked the idea, and it became a top-secret mission because the U.S. government did not want Russia to find out about it.

On July 23, 1958, Commander Anderson and his crew of 115 men set sail in the *Nautilus* from Pearl Harbor, Hawaii. They sailed north and eventually reached the Bering Strait, which is right between Alaska and eastern Russia. They had to be careful to not be seen by any Russian ships and also to not crash into the huge ice chunks floating in the strait.

After sailing through the Bering Strait and then the Chukchi Sea, the *Nautilus* reached Point Barrow, Alaska, which is farther north than any other place in the United States. On August 1, 1958, the *Nautilus* submerged (dove down) into the water near Point Barrow and headed toward the North Pole. It soon entered the Arctic Ocean and began sailing underneath the Arctic ice sheets. If anything went wrong with their submarine, all of the men on board would be in great danger.

Commander Anderson had spent a lot of time looking at maps of the Arctic region, and he had a special **device** called a gyro compass to help him know their location. At 11:15 p.m. on August 3, the *Nautilus* became the first submarine to sail under the North Pole. Commander Anderson and his crew celebrated and continued on their voyage.

Two days later, on August 5, the *Nautilus* sailed into the Atlantic Ocean and rose back up to the surface of the water off the coast of Greenland. Commander Anderson and his men soon returned to the United States, and crowds of people cheered for them when they arrived in New York Harbor in New York City. President Eisenhower gave the crew of the *Nautilus* the Presidential Unit Citation, which is a special award given to groups of soldiers, pilots, and sailors in the U.S. military who have done extraordinary and brave things.

Many people around the world were amazed by the voyage of the *Nautilus*, which was one of the greatest adventures in history. The United States became a more powerful country because of this accomplishment and also had a way to secretly reach the northern coast of Russia by sending submarines underneath the ice sheets of the Arctic Ocean. (You can learn more about the competition between the United States and Russia in my book *U.S. History Bites*.)

Commander William Anderson (center, seated) and his crew in the Nautilus during its voyage under the North Pole

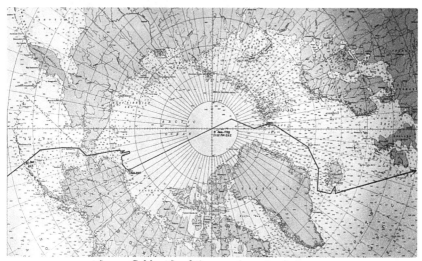

Map of the Nautilus submarine's voyage

REVIEW BITES

VOCABULARY

Satellite – an object that is sent into outer space to gather information about different areas of the world

Submarines – boats that can sail underwater

Device – a small machine or tool

FUN FACT

The *Nautilus* was named after the submarine in the book *20,000 Leagues Under the Sea*, which was written by a French author named Jules Verne and published in 1870. It tells the story of Captain Nemo and Professor Aronnax, who sail around the world in a submarine called the *Nautilus*.

REVIEW QUESTIONS

1. What was the first nuclear-powered submarine?

2. Who was the commander of the *Nautilus?*

3. What did the *Nautilus* pass under during its voyage?

Yuri Gagarin's Journey Into Space
1961

Yuri Gagarin inside Vostok 3KA, ready to take off into space

After Russia launched the first satellite into outer space in 1957 and started the Space Race with the United States, both countries wanted to be the first to send a person into space. In 1960, Russia began the Vostok **program** to achieve this goal, and they chose a group of twenty pilots to begin training to fly into space. (Russia called these people cosmonauts, while the United States called them astronauts.) One of the Russian pilots chosen was Yuri Gagarin.

Yuri Gagarin was born in 1934 near the city of Gzhatsk, Russia. When he was a teenager, he became interested in flying and attended a school where he learned how to fly an airplane. In 1957, he joined the Russian Air Force and spent two years flying fighter planes and testing new equipment.

In 1960, Gagarin was chosen to become one of the first cosmonauts as part of the Vostok program, and he began training to fly into outer space. The leader of the Vostok program was a man named Sergei Korolev, and he became close friends with Gagarin and decided that Gagarin would be the first cosmonaut to fly to space.

On the morning of April 12, 1961, Gagarin got into his small spaceship, called the Vostok 3KA, which was attached to a big rocket. At 9:07 a.m., he took off from the city of Leninsk in the present-day country of Kazakhstan. The rocket pushed him into the sky, and he passed through Earth's **atmosphere** and became the first person to enter outer space.

Gagarin could see planet Earth beneath him and the blackness of space all around. Far away, the Sun was shining brightly, and he was careful not to look at it so that he did not hurt his eyes. Over the next hour and a half, he **orbited** the Earth at a speed of around 17,000 miles per hour and flew over the Pacific Ocean, South America, and Africa. Gagarin then began his descent, which is when a spaceship returns to Earth. When he was at a height of 20,000 feet in the sky, he was shot out of his spaceship by a special machine called an ejection seat, and he opened up his **parachute** to float the rest of the way to the ground. Around two hours after taking off from Earth, Gagarin landed in the middle of a farm field near the city of Saratov, Russia.

Yuri Gagarin became very famous for his journey into space, which was one of the greatest adventures in history. Sadly, in 1968, he died in a plane crash near Moscow, the capital city of Russia, while flying for the Russian Air Force.

Model of the Vostok 3KA spaceship © de:Benutzer:HPH (refer to page 209)

Yuri Gagarin standing in a parade car in
Moscow, Russia, after his journey into outer space

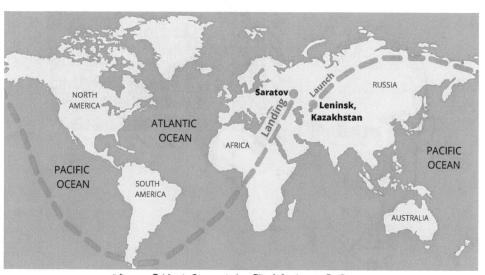

Map of Yuri Gagarin's flight by L.B. Dugan

REVIEW BITES

VOCABULARY

Program – a set of activities or jobs

Atmosphere – a layer of gases, such as oxygen and nitrogen, that surround planet Earth

Orbited – traveled around a planet

Parachute – a large cloth that people attach to themselves with cords to help them float slowly to the ground

FUN FACT

During his journey to space, Yuri Gagarin talked over a radio with Sergei Korolev back in Russia. When he first took off from Earth, Gagarin shouted "Poyekhali!" into the radio, which means "Let's go!" in the Russian language.

REVIEW QUESTIONS

1. What was the Vostok program?

2. Who was the first person
to enter outer space?

3. What did Yuri Gagarin use to
float safely to the ground?

1. A program Russia began in order to achieve the goal of
sending a person into space 2. Yuri Gagarin 3. A parachute

Apollo 11 Mission to the Moon 1969

Astronaut Buzz Aldrin on the moon

After the Russian cosmonaut Yuri Gagarin became the first person to go to outer space in April of 1961, many people around the world thought that Russia was beating the United States in the Space Race. On May 25, 1961, U.S. President John F. Kennedy made a speech in which he said that the United States should try to achieve the goal of landing a person on the Moon before the end of the 1960s. This would not only be a great accomplishment, but it would also help the United States win the Space Race.

NASA (the National Aeronautics and Space Administration) was in charge of sending U.S. astronauts into space, and they started the Apollo program to accomplish President Kennedy's goal. Between 1961-1968, they launched many flights into space to test the rockets and equipment that would be needed for a person to land on the Moon. The Moon is about 240,000 miles from Earth, and there are many places on the Moon with mountains and craters where it would be dangerous to land. NASA chose an area on the Moon called the Mare Tranquillitatis, which is flat and safe to land on.

In 1969, NASA was ready to launch Apollo 11, which was the eleventh flight of the Apollo program. The three astronauts aboard Apollo 11 were Neil Armstrong, Buzz Aldrin, and Michael Collins. The Apollo 11 spaceship was made up of three main parts: the command **module** (where the astronauts rode), the lunar module (which would separate from the command module and land on the Moon), and a main rocket (which would push the spaceship off the ground and toward the Moon).

On the morning of July 16, 1969, Apollo 11 launched from Cape Kennedy, Florida, and flew into the sky and out of Earth's atmosphere. The next part of the flight was from Earth to the Moon. Over the next three days, the astronauts flew through outer space and filmed parts of their journey with a camera so people on Earth could see it on television.

On July 19, 1969, the Apollo 11 spaceship reached the Moon, and the command and lunar modules separated from each other. Michael Collins stayed in the command module, while Neil Armstrong and Buzz Aldrin got in the lunar module (called the *Eagle*) and began flying down toward the surface of the Moon. Around 9:00 p.m. on July 20, 1969, they landed in the Mare Tranquillitatis area, and Armstrong spoke these now-famous words over a radio to NASA: "The *Eagle* has landed." Soon after, he got out of the *Eagle* and stepped onto the Moon. Aldrin also came out, and together, they explored parts of the Moon, grabbed some rocks and dirt to bring back to Earth, and also placed an American flag in the ground.

After spending many hours on the Moon, they took off and flew back to the command module. It took two and a half days for the astronauts to return, and on July 24, they entered Earth's atmosphere and splashed down in the Pacific Ocean, where the ship USS *Hornet* was waiting to pick them up.

The Apollo 11 mission to the Moon was one of the greatest adventures of all time, and because it was successful, the United States won the Space Race against Russia. Neil Armstrong, Buzz Aldrin, and Michael Collins became known as heroes around the world, especially Armstrong because he was the first person to walk on the Moon.

Apollo 11 taking off

The Eagle returning to the command module

Apollo 11 JUL 69
Mare Tranquillitatis
0.67416°N 23.47314°E
LM: 21.6 hours EVA: 2.5 hours

Apollo 12 NOV 69
Oceanus Procellarum
3.0128°S 23.4219°W
LM: 31.5 hours EVA: 7.8 hours

Apollo 14 FEB 71
Fra Mauro Highlands
3.64589°S 17.47194°W
LM: 33.5 hours EVA: 9.4 hours

Apollo 15 AUG 71
Hadley Rille
26.13239°N 3.63330°E
LM: 66.9 hours EVA: 19.1 hours

Apollo 16 APR 72
Descartes Highlands
8.9734°S 15.5011°E
LM: 71.0 hours EVA: 20.2 hours

Apollo 17 DEC 72
Taurus-Littrow Valley
20.1911°N 30.7655°E
LM: 75.0 hours EVA: 22.1 hours

Apollo Landing Sites

Map of the moon landing sites of several Apollo flights

VOCABULARY

Module – part of a spaceship that can be separated from the rest of the spaceship and flown by itself

FUN FACT

When Neil Armstrong first stepped onto the Moon, he said this over the radio to NASA: "That's one small step for man, one giant leap for mankind." He meant to say, "That's one small step for a man, one giant leap for mankind," but accidentally forgot to say "a" before the word "man."

REVIEW QUESTIONS

1. What was the Apollo program?

2. Who were the three astronauts on the Apollo 11 mission?

3. Who was the first person to walk on the Moon?

Dr. Ballard's Discovery of the *Titanic* 1985

Hull (front) of the Titanic *wreck underwater*

The *Titanic* was an **ocean liner** owned by a British ship company called White Star Line. When it was built in the early 1900s, it was the largest ship in the world (882 feet long), and people said that it was unsinkable because of how it was built. However, on April 14, 1912, while sailing from England to the United States, the *Titanic* hit a huge iceberg in the middle of the Atlantic Ocean and sank in about two hours. More than 1,500 passengers died, and the story of the *Titanic* became well known around the world. Many people wondered where the **wreck** of the ship was located.

Robert Ballard was born in 1942 in the state of Kansas and grew up in San Diego, California. When he was a young boy, he loved to go scuba diving in the ocean. He eventually joined the U.S. Navy and worked with the Woods Hole Oceanographic Institute in Massachusetts to help the Navy learn more about using machines underwater. During the 1970s, Ballard earned a doctorate degree from the University of Rhode Island and received the title "Doctor" (Dr.) before his name. He also explored parts of the Atlantic and Pacific Oceans in a submersible (small submarine) called *Alvin*.

Dr. Ballard had thought about finding the wreck of the *Titanic* for many years, but he needed a lot of money to try to find it. He talked to the U.S. Navy about his idea, and they said that he could use the U.S. ship *Knorr* for his expedition, but only if he first went on two missions for the Navy. The Navy wanted to get information about two submarines called the USS *Thresher* and the USS *Scorpion*, both of which had sunk in the Atlantic Ocean during the 1960s.

In 1984, Dr. Ballard and his crew on the *Knorr* went to the place where the Thresher had sunk and sent a submersible called *Argo* down to take pictures of it. Several months later, in August of 1985, Dr. Ballard set off again in the *Knorr* and sailed to a point southwest of the Azores Islands in the Atlantic Ocean, where the *Scorpion* submarine had sunk. As soon as the *Argo* finished taking pictures and video of the *Scorpion*, Dr. Ballard sailed the *Knorr* toward the area where the *Titanic* had sunk seventy-three years earlier. The problem was he only had twelve days to find the wreck because the Navy needed the *Knorr* for another mission.

Dr. Ballard and his crew arrived at a place in the Atlantic Ocean about one thousand miles east of Boston, Massachusetts, and they sent the *Argo* down into the water to start searching for the *Titanic*. Over the next several days, the *Argo* took video of the bottom of the ocean, but there was no sign of the massive ship.

Amazingly, around 1:00 a.m. on September 1, 1985, they saw a **boiler** from the *Titanic* on the camera screen of the *Argo*. The next day, they found the ship itself at almost 13,000 feet underwater. Dr. Ballard and his crew were very excited, but also very sad when they thought about all the people who had died on the *Titanic*. They used the *Argo* to take many pictures of the wreck, and soon after, they sailed back to the United States.

Dr. Robert Ballard became famous for his discovery of the *Titanic*, which was one of the greatest adventures in history. Since 1985, other people have gone down to the wreck of the ship to find and bring back **artifacts** from it.

Dr. Robert Ballard in a submersible

The Alvin submersible underwater

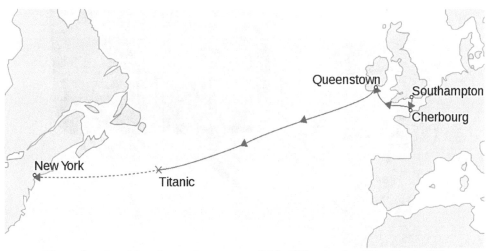

Map showing the planned voyage of the Titanic to New York City (the "X" marks the location where it sunk into the Atlantic Ocean)

REVIEW BITES

VOCABULARY

Ocean liner – a large ship that carries passengers across an ocean

Wreck – what is left of a ship, car, or airplane after an accident

Boiler – a machine that burns coal or fuel so that a ship's engine can run

Artifacts – things owned or used by people from history

FUN FACT

After he discovered the wreck of the *Titanic*, Dr. Robert Ballard went on to discover wrecks of other famous ships, such as the Nazi German battleship *Bismarck* and PT-109, which was President John F. Kennedy's ship when he fought in the U.S. Navy during World War II.

REVIEW QUESTIONS

1. What year did the *Titanic* sink into the Atlantic Ocean?

2. What was the name of the submersible that Dr. Robert Ballard used to take pictures and video of the *Titanic*?

3. How deep underwater was the wreck of the *Titanic*?

Rob Hall (left) and Gary Ball at Mt. Everest base camp (© Jan Arnold)

The Seven Summits are the highest mountains on each continent: Mt. Everest (29,032 feet, Asia), Mt. Denali (20,310 ft., North America), Mt. Elbrus (18,510 ft., Europe), Mt. Kilimanjaro (19,341 ft., Africa), Mt. Kosciuszko (7,310 ft., Australia), Mt. Aconcagua (22,841 ft., South America), and Mt. Vinson (16,050 ft., Antarctica). The first person to climb all Seven Summits was Richard Bass from the United States, and he did it in two years from 1983-1985. A few years later, an American climber named Geoffrey Tabin climbed them in twenty-one months, which was the fastest anyone had ever done it. There were two climbers from New Zealand who were determined to beat this record: Rob Hall and Gary Ball.

Rob Hall was born in New Zealand in 1961, and he became **passionate** about climbing when he was a teenager. He climbed in the Southern Alps Mountain Range in New Zealand and in the Himalayas. Gary Ball was born in New Zealand in 1953, and he also loved to climb and eventually began working as a guide in the mountains of Antarctica.

Hall and Ball met each other in 1987 in the city of Christchurch, New Zealand, and became friends. They decided to become a team and climb together. In 1988, they climbed K2 in the country of Pakistan, which is the second tallest mountain in the world (but not the tallest on the continent of Asia). Two years later, on May 10, 1990, they reached the top of Mt. Everest, along with their friend Apa Sherpa from Nepal.

After they got back to New Zealand, Hall and Ball decided to go on an expedition to climb the Seven Summits in seven months, which would be a new record for the fastest anyone had ever done it before. Since they had already climbed Mt. Everest on May 10, they had to climb the other six mountains by December 10, 1990, in order to accomplish their goal. They made plans, got supplies ready, and in mid-June, set off to Alaska, where they climbed Mt. Denali in nice weather.

The two climbers then went back to New Zealand to rest and prepare for their next journey. They needed money to pay for their trips, and an electric company named Powerbuild agreed to give them the money if they called their expedition the Powerbuild Seven Summits Expedition. Near the beginning of August, Hall and Ball traveled to Russia and climbed Mt. Elbrus, and after that, they flew to the country of Tanzania in Africa to climb Mt. Kilimanjaro. The two men reached the top of the mountain very quickly and climbed through rainforests and over glaciers on their way up.

The next mountain on their **itinerary** was Mt. Kosciuszko in Australia, which is small and usually easy to climb. However, they climbed it during Australia's winter season, and while they were going up the mountain, Hall and Ball got caught in a snowstorm and had a very difficult time reaching the summit.

Before they could go on to their next mountain in South America, they had to wait for the summer season in South America so that they would hopefully have nice weather. In November, they left New Zealand and headed to Mt. Aconcagua in Argentina, which is known as the "Mountain of Death" because so many people die trying to climb it. On November 20, they made it to the top and back down, but as they were walking away from the mountain, they were almost buried in a **mudslide**.

After Mt. Aconcagua, the two men only had one mountain left, and on December 4, they left South America and flew to Antarctica to climb Mt. Vinson. They were trapped in a blizzard on the mountain for two days, but on December 10, the weather became sunny and clear. That same day, they reached the top of Mt. Vinson just hours before their **deadline** of seven months.

Hall and Ball's Seven Summits Expedition was one of the greatest adventures in history, and they became some of the most famous climbers in the world. Sadly, in 1993, Gary Ball died of a sickness called pulmonary edema on Mt. Dhaulagiri in Nepal, and in 1996, Rob Hall died on Mt. Everest after he tried to save another climber's life.

Mt. Denali in North America

Mt. Elbrus in Europe

Elephants in front of Mt. Kilimanjaro in Africa

Mt. Kosciuszko in Australia © Pee Tern (refer to page 209)

Mt. Aconcagua in South America

Mt. Vinson in Antarctica © Christian Stangl (refer to page 209)

Map of the Seven Summits by L.B. Dugan

VOCABULARY

Passionate – very excited about something

Itinerary – a schedule of places where someone has planned to go

Mudslide – a large pile of falling mud and rocks

Deadline – the date and/or time by which a project has to be finished

FUN FACT

Rob Hall met his future wife, Jan Arnold, on one of his expeditions in the Himalayas, and for their first "date," they climbed to the top of Mt. Denali together. They got married in 1992 and eventually had a daughter named Sarah. Over the course of many years, Jan climbed the rest of the Seven Summits, including Mt. Kilimanjaro, which she and Sarah climbed together in 2011.

REVIEW QUESTIONS

1. What are the Seven Summits?

2. What country were
Rob Hall and Gary Ball from?

3. How long did it take Hall and Ball
to climb the Seven Summits?

1. The highest mountains on each continent
2. New Zealand 3. Seven months

TO THE READER

Congratulations! You have finished reading *Great Adventures History Bites.*

I hope you have enjoyed it and that you will continue to learn more about incredible adventures and explorers from history.

~Solomon

GLOSSARY

A

A.D. – a term that stands for the Latin words *Anno Domini*, which mean "in the year of our Lord"; this term refers to all dates after the birth of Jesus Christ

Advantages – things that help a person to accomplish something faster and more easily than someone else

Ancient – very old

Arabic – from the land of Arabia (present-day Middle East)

Arrested – when a person is taken by the police or military and is not allowed to go free for a certain amount of time

Artifacts – things owned or used by people from history

Atmosphere – a layer of gasses, such as oxygen and nitrogen, that surround planet Earth

Banished – forced to leave one's home or country as a punishment

Biology – the study of how humans, plants, and animals live

Boiler – a machine that burns coal or fuel so that a ship's engine can run

Businessman – a man who owns a company that sells things to people

Canyon – a deep, long valley between mountains or hills

Cavalry – the part of the military in which soldiers ride on horses

Civil engineer – a person who designs plans for bridges, roads, and buildings

Clubs – groups of people who get together to do activities

Committee – a group of people who make decisions for a business, project, or expedition

Companions — friends on a journey

Continents — very large areas of land; there are seven continents in the world: North America, South America, Europe, Africa, Asia, Australia, and Antarctica

Convert — cause someone to change their religious beliefs

Corps — a group of soldiers or explorers

Crew — a group of sailors who work together on a ship

Criminals — people who break the law and have to go to prison

Cultures — the customs and traditions of a people

Currents — water that moves in a specific direction

D

Deadline — the date and/or time by which a project has to be finished

Deserted — left alone

Determined — when a person does not give up and

tries hard to accomplish something

Device – a small machine or tool

Eccentric – unique in a strange way

Encountered – came across

Equator – a line drawn on world maps and globes that goes all the way around planet Earth and separates the northern part of the planet from the southern part

Exhaustion – when a person is very tired and his/her body becomes extremely weak

Extraordinary – unusual and amazing

Fled – ran away or escaped from

Floes – large chunks of ice that float on top of water

Foreigners – people from a different country

Frostbite – when a person loses feeling in their

hands, feet, and face, and their skin changes color because of very cold temperatures

Geography – the study of areas of land on the Earth

Geologist – someone who studies water, land, and rocks

Glacier – a large chunk of ice that forms near mountains

Hemisphere – one of the four main areas of planet Earth, which are: northern, southern, western, and eastern hemispheres

Horizon – the line in the distance where the sky and ground meet

Hospitable – when someone is friendly to strangers and is willing to share their home and food with others

Hurricane – a huge and violent storm that usually forms over the Caribbean Sea and the Gulf of Mexico

Igloo — a small, dome-shaped house made out of hard snow and ice

Infection — when germs get into a person's body and cause them to become sick

Inhabited — lived in/on by people

Itinerary — a schedule of places where someone has planned to go

Journalist — someone who writes articles for a newspaper

Journals — notebooks that people write in to keep track of things they do

License — a government document that a person needs in order to do things like drive a car or fly an airplane

Mast — a pole in the center of a boat that a sail is attached to so that wind can blow the boat forward

Merchants – people who buy and sell goods, such as clothing, jewelry, and food

Mine – a place where things like gold, coal, and salt are dug out of the ground

Missionary – someone who goes to other countries to tell people about their religion

Module – part of a spaceship that can be separated from the rest of the spaceship and flown by itself

Mormons – followers of Mormonism, which is a religion started by Joseph Smith (you can learn about Joseph Smith in my book *In/Famous People History Bites Volume I*)

Mudslide – a large pile of falling mud and rocks

Mutiny – a crew's rebellion against a sea captain

Mysterious – cannot be explained

N

Navigate – figure out the right way to go in order to reach a destination

Navigator – someone who uses maps to figure out which way to go during a trip

Navy – a group of ships that is part of a country's military

Observed – watched from a distance

Ocean liner – a large ship that carries passengers across an ocean

Orbited – traveled around a planet

Oxygen – a gas in the air that people need to breathe in order to stay alive

Parachute – a large cloth that people attach to themselves with cords to help them float slowly to the ground

Passage – a waterway in the middle of an area of land that connects one body of water to another

Passionate – very excited about something

Pier – a platform that starts on land and goes out into the water

Prestigious – respected; important

Presume - when a person believes that something is true, but does not know for sure

Priest - a person who offers sacrifices to God or gods as part of their religion

Program - a set of activities or jobs

Progress - movement toward to finishing a project or accomplishing something

Provinces - areas of land that are parts of a country (similar to states)

R

Raids - attacks in which people capture land and steal important items

Rank - a position in the military

Rapids - fast-moving parts of a river

Region - an area of land

Repairs - fixes to a machine to make it work properly

Representative - a person who speaks or does business for a leader/ruler

Route – a road or path that people travel on

Runway – a long, smooth area of ground at an airport that planes take off from and land on

Sarcastically – when a person says something in a way that is meant to make fun of another person

Satellite – an object that is sent into outer space to gather information about different areas of the world

Secretary – a person who helps someone write letters and keep track of his/her schedule

Slave trade – the practice of buying and selling people to work as slaves

Sponsor – pay for

Starvation – when someone dies because they do not have enough food to eat

Submarine – boats that can sail underwater

Surveyor – someone who explores areas of land and makes maps of those areas

Telegram – a message that is sent using a machine called the telegraph

Terrorized – scared people by hurting them and/or by destroying their home and belongings

Tides – changes in the height of the oceans; high tide is when water levels are higher and cover more of a beach, and low tide is when water levels are lower and more of a beach can be seen

Tomb – a place where a dead person is buried

Translators – people who explain the meaning of a language to someone who does not know how to speak it

Treasurer – a person who keeps track of the money for a group

Tribes – groups of people who live together

Tributaries – small rivers that flow into larger rivers

Turquoise – a bright bluish-green color

U

Unstable – when something is not strong or steady

W

Whirlpool – an area in a river or ocean where water swirls around and pulls things into it

Wilderness – a large area of land where very few people live (or none at all)

Wreck – what is left of a ship, car, or airplane after an accident

WORKS CITED

1. Page 69 – "The lands they traveled through were filled with many scary animals, and lions sometimes came near their camp at night." Martin Dugard, *Into Africa: The Epic Adventures of Stanley and Livingstone* (Doubleday, 2003), pg. 248

2. Page 83 – "While he was bicycling through the state of Nevada, Thomas Stevens encountered a mountain lion that was getting ready to attack him. Stevens shot a bullet at the lion, and even though he missed, the lion ran back into the woods." Thomas Stevens, *Around the World on a Bicycle: From San Francisco to Teheran* (New York: Charles Scribner's Sons, 1894), pp. 39–40

3. Page 135 – "In his book *The Long Walk*, Slavomir Rawicz wrote that while he and his companions were crossing the Himalayan Mountains, they saw two tall animals that looked like Abominable Snowmen, which are big, scary creatures that some people believe live in the Himalayas." Slavomir Rawicz, *The Long Walk: A Gamble for Life* (Harper and Brothers: Publishers New York, 1956), pp. 232–234

4. Page 180 – "Hall and Ball met each other in 1987 in the city of Christchurch, New Zealand, and became friends." Colin Monteath, *Hall & Ball: Kiwi Mountaineers: From Mount Cook to Everest* (Hedgehog House, 1998), pg. 68

5. Page 180 – "**They decided to become a team and climb together. In 1988, they climbed K2 in the country of Pakistan...**" ibid., pg. 9

6. Pages 180-181 – "**They made plans, got supplies ready, and in mid-June, set off to Alaska, where they climbed Mt. Denali in nice weather.**" ibid., pg. 97

7. Page 181 – "**The two climbers then went back to New Zealand to rest and prepare for their next journey.**" ibid., pg. 97

8. Page 181 – "**They needed money to pay for their trips, and an electric company named Powerbuild agreed to give them the money if they called their expedition the Powerbuild Seven Summits Expedition.**" ibid., pg. 97

9. Page 181 – "**The two men reached the top of the mountain very quickly and climbed through rainforests and over glaciers on their way up.**" ibid., pg. 98

10. Page 181 – "**The next mountain on their** itinerary **was Mt. Kosciuszko in Australia...**" ibid., pg. 98

11. Page 181 – "**...while they were going up the mountain, Hall and Ball got caught in a snowstorm and had a very difficult time reaching the summit.**" ibid., pg. 98

12. Page 181 – "**Before they could go on to their next mountain in South America, they had to wait for the summer season in South America so that they would hopefully have nice weather.**" ibid., pg. 98

13. Page 181 – "In November, they left New Zealand and headed to Mt. Aconcagua in Argentina..." ibid., pg. 98

14. Page 182 – "On November 20, they made it to the top and back down, but as they were walking away from the mountain, they were almost buried in a mudslide." ibid., pg. 98

15. Page 182 – "After Mt. Aconcagua, the two men only had one mountain left, and on December 4, they left South America and flew to Antarctica to climb Mt. Vinson." ibid., pg. 99

16. Page 182 – "They were trapped in a blizzard on the mountain for two days, but on December 10, the weather became sunny and clear." ibid., pg. 99

17. Page 182 – "That same day, they reached the top of Mt. Vinson just hours before their deadline of seven months." ibid., pg. 99

IMAGE CREDITS

The following are links to licenses referred to in these image credits:

CC BY 2.0 - https://creativecommons.org/licenses/by/2.0/legalcode
CC BY-SA 2.0 - https://creativecommons.org/licenses/by-sa/2.0/legalcode
CC BY-SA 3.0 - https://creativecommons.org/licenses/by-sa/3.0/legalcode
CC BY 4.0 - https://creativecommons.org/licenses/by/4.0/deed.en
CC BY-SA 4.0 - https://creativecommons.org/licenses/by-sa/4.0/legalcode

1. Picture of an area of land in present-day Pakistan that was once part of the Silk Road (page 9) - "Tupopdan Peak" by Shahid Mehmood is licensed under CC BY-SA 4.0. Link to the image: https://www.theatlantic.com/photo/2017/11/a-photo-trip-along-the-ancient-silk-road/546767/. A portion of the border has been cropped on the bottom, left side, and right side of the original image. Shahid Mehmood has not endorsed use of image.

2. Map of Marco Polo's journey (page 10) - "Route of Marco Polo" by SY is licensed under CC BY-SA 4.0. Link to the image: https://commons.wikimedia.org/wiki/File:Route_of_Marco_Polo.png. A small portion of the border has been

cropped on the left side and right side of the original image. SY has not endorsed use of image.

3. Map of Christopher Columbus's voyages to the New World (page 16) – "Viajes de colon en.svg" by Viajes_de_colon.svg: Phirosiberia is licensed under CC BY-SA 3.0. Link to the image: https://commons.wikimedia.org/wiki/File:Viajes_de_colon_en.svg. No changes have been made to the original image. Viajes_de_colon.svg: Phirosiberia has not endorsed use of image.

4. Map of the first voyage around the world (page 28) – "Magellan Elcano Circumnavigation-en.svg" by Magellan_Elcano_Circumnavigation-fr.svg: Sémhur is licensed under CC BY-SA 3.0. Link to the image: https://commons.wikimedia.org/wiki/File:Magellan_Elcano_Circumnavigation-en.svg. No changes have been made to the original image. Magellan_Elcano_Circumnavigation-fr.svg: Sémhur has not endorsed use of image.

5. Map of Captain Cook's voyages around the world (page 40) – "Cook Three Voyages 59.png" by Jon Platek is licensed under CC BY-SA 3.0. Link to the image: https://commons.wikimedia.org/wiki/File:Cook_Three_Voyages_59.png. No changes have been made to the original image. Jon Platek has not endorsed use of image.

6. Map of the English Channel (page 76) – "Map of the English Channel and coasts.png" by Serial Number 54129 is licensed under CC BY-SA 4.0. Link to the image: https://commons.wikimedia.org/wiki/File:Map_of_the_English_Channel_and_coasts.png. A portion of the border has been

cropped on the top, bottom, and right side of the original image. Serial Number 54129 has not endorsed use of image.

7. Map of Thomas Stevens's bicycle journey (page 82) – "Thomas-Stevens's-bicycle-journey-EN.png" by Benutzer: Dravot is licensed under CC BY-SA 3.0. Link to the image: https://commons.wikimedia.org/wiki/File:Thomas-Stevens%27s-bicycle-journey-EN.png. A small portion of the border has been cropped on the bottom, left side, and right side of the original image. Benutzer: Dravot has not endorsed use of image.

8. Map of Shackleton's Antarctic expedition (page 110) – "Imperial Trans-Antarctic Expedition, map and timeline. svg" by Luca Ferrario, DensityDesign Research Lab is licensed under CC BY-SA 4.0. Link to the image: https://commons.wikimedia.org/wiki/File:Imperial_Trans-Antarctic_Expedition,_map_and_timeline.svg. A portion of the border has been cropped on the top, bottom, left side, and right side of the original image. DensityDesign Research Lab has not endorsed use of image.

9. Map of Amelia Earhart's final flight (page 128) – "Amelia Earhart flight route.svg" by Hellerick is licensed under CC BY-SA 3.0. Link to the image: https://commons.wikimedia.org/wiki/File:Amelia_Earhart_flight_route.svg. No changes have been made to the original image. Hellerick has not endorsed use of image.

10. Picture of Lake Namtso (page 134) – "NamTso scene.jpg" by Reurinkjan is licensed under CC BY 2.0. Link to the image: https://commons.wikimedia.org/wiki/File:NamTso_scene.jpg.

A small portion of the border has been cropped on the top of the original image. Reurinkjan has not endorsed use of image.

11. Picture of the Makassar Strait (page 140) – "Pulau Aur (Kalimantan Selatan).jpg" by Marwan Mohamad is licensed under CC BY-SA 4.0. Link to the image: https://commons.wikimedia.org/wiki/File:Pulau_Aur_(Kalimantan_Selatan).jpg. A portion of the border has been cropped on the top of the original image. Marwan Mohamad has not endorsed use of image.

12. Picture of Thor Heyerdahl (page 143) – "Thor Heyerdahl – L0061 934Fo30141701190044.jpg" by Bjørn Fjørtoft is licensed under CC BY 4.0. Link to the image: https://commons.wikimedia.org/wiki/File:Thor_Heyerdahl_-_L0061_934Fo30141701190044.jpg. A portion of the border has been cropped on the top, bottom, left side, and right side of the original image. Bjørn Fjørtoft has not endorsed use of image.

13. Picture of the *Kon-Tiki* raft (page 146) – "Expedition Kon-Tiki 1947. Across the Pacific. (8765728430).jpg" by Nasjonalbiblioteket is licensed under CC BY 2.0. Link to the image: https://commons.wikimedia.org/wiki/File:Expedition_Kon-Tiki_1947._Across_the_Pacific._(8765728430).jpg. A small portion of the border has been cropped on the bottom and left side of the original image. Nasjonalbiblioteket has not endorsed use of image.

14. Picture of Edmund Hillary and Tenzing Norgay (page 152) – "Edmund Hillary and Tenzing Norgay.jpg" by Jamling Tenzing

Norgay is licensed under CC BY-SA 3.0. Link to the image: https://commons.wikimedia.org/wiki/File:Edmund_Hillary_and_Tenzing_Norgay.jpg. A small portion of the border has been cropped on the top and bottom of the original image. Jamling Tenzing Norgay has not endorsed use of image.

15. Picture of a model of the Vostok 3KA spaceship (page 163) - "Vostok spacecraft.jpg" by de:Benutzer:HPH is licensed under CC BY-SA 3.0. Link to the image: https://commons.wikimedia.org/wiki/File:Vostok_spacecraft.jpg. No changes have been made to the original image. de:Benutzer:HPH has not endorsed use of image.

16. Picture of Mt. Kosciuszko (page 183) - "Towards Kosciuszko from Kangaroo Ridge in winter.jpg" by Pee Tern is licensed under CC BY-SA 3.0. Link to the image: https://commons.wikimedia.org/wiki/File:Towards_Kosciuszko_from_Kangaroo_Ridge_in_winter.jpg. A portion of the border has been cropped on the top of the original image. Pee Tern has not endorsed use of image.

17. Picture of Mt. Vinson (page 184) - "Mount Vinson from NW at Vinson Plateau by Christian Stangl (flickr).jpg" by Christian Stangl is licensed under CC BY 2.0. Link to the image: https://commons.wikimedia.org/wiki/File:Mount_Vinson_from_NW_at_Vinson_Plateau_by_Christian_Stangl_(flickr).jpg. A portion of the border has been cropped on the top and bottom of the original image. Christian Stangl has not endorsed use of image.